Master of Pieces

By Marlee Bruno

I have written this book for the sole purpose of paying off my student loans. I have asked President Obama for assistance in this matter, but he has assured me via email that he has already put several bills into place to aid in my situation. I have participated in such programs for years, and I am still broke. Thank you for responding, though, Barack. That was really decent of you.

Though it may not be reflected in this book, I swear I have a master's degree in medicine. Thank you for your purchase. You are supporting a good cause.

This book is dedicated to Tarah, the only constant in my life. Without you, I would not have been able to have made it through half of what has occurred here. You just called me to tell me that you passed the physical portion of the police test, but not without pissing your pants on your last lap of the run. I am so proud of you. You are the baddest bitch.

I would also like to thank my seventeen-year-old niece, Hailee, who was the first editor of this book (at age fifteen). Although she is a very mature seventeen, she is now scarred for life, but she would have been anyway because I am, after all, her aunt.

Thank you also to Jade Lace for your excellent photography skills and for designing the cover of this book. You have a true gift. Keep shining.

In loving memory of Marcina, a wild and beautiful woman who told me to march to the beat of my own different drummer. If only she could see me now.

And Corey, a handsome man with a tortured soul who forced me to believe that I was a diamond in the rough.

"She brought out the storm in people, because she knew wherever there were dark skies and wild winds, lied a truth. A truth that described how much love one can leave behind the moment they accept all the pain they have lived.

And that is all she ever wanted. For everyone around her to embrace their storms and make them fall in love with their own violent winds."

-R.M. Drake

Foreword

It is 3:55pm. I have just walked in through the ambulance bay to start my shift. I look to my left to find an elderly woman and a very attractive young man standing in the hall. They appear to be very nervous. There are two chairs sitting up against the wall, but they are empty. I imagine they were put there so that these two could sit in them, but they are too anxious to sit.

Me: "What's the deal with the old lady and the hot guy in the hall?"

Nurse: "They're with room 5. He came in complaining of chest pain and deteriorated quickly, so they're in there tubing him now. She's the wife. Hot dude is the son."

Me: "That sucks. What's it look like? He have a history?"

Nurse: "Healthy guy with only hypertension as far as he knew. Came in talking. Went down fast. He just got here a few minutes ago. Labs are normal so far. We're scanning him."

Me: "Cool. Let me know what you find."

I walk in to see if I can offer any help with the intubation. They've got it all under control. The intubation went very smoothly. I see that there are four new charts in the rack, so I pick one up. Room 9: "Psych problems". Just as I'm reading the complaint, a young man bolts out of the door of our designated psychiatric room and runs toward the nurse's station. He's wearing his gown, but it's not tied shut in the back, so it's flapping in the wind as he runs, showing his bare ass. He doesn't seem to mind.

Psych patient: "You fucks better let me go! I'm fine! I'm not gonna do it! I'm not gonna fucking kill myself today, OK!?"

I turn to my nurse, "Oh. Looks like I picked up the right chart". She grins.

Me: "Hey sweetness. I'm Marlee. I'm the physician assistant here. I'll be the one taking care of you today. I just got here, honey, so if you'll give me two minutes, I'll be right in to talk with you, and we'll see if we can get something worked out, cool?" I calmly motion for him step back into his room.

Psych patient: "Yeah OK. But hurry up. I swear I'll fucking leave this place!"

I give the nurse a verbal order to give him 20mg of Geodon intramuscularly if he gets any more out of control. Geodon is a commonly used drug that we use to treat acute agitation in the emergency setting. Some people take it daily for psychosis. At this point, I also tell the unit secretary to call security. I have just driven about an hour and forty minutes to be here. I'm working in different ERs all over the state, so I travel pretty far some days. I peek over at the family members for room 5. They now appear agitated, probably because of the naked ass they've just seen and the foul mouth they've just heard. I'm sure they weren't expecting

6

this sort of behavior after they've just had to watch us emergently put their loved one on a ventilator. I try and offer a half-smile, but it doesn't seem to make a difference.

Mr. Donahue wants to kill himself because he caught his girlfriend cheating several months prior. They had decided they would try and make it work anyway, but apparently she cheated again. I offer my empathy to Mr. Donahue, but he quickly tells me that he would also like to kill his girlfriend today. This is a big "no-no" in the emergency department. Mr. Donahue has just admitted that he is homicidal, so he will not be leaving our facility today. He will be held against his will and court-ordered to have intensive psychiatric treatment. I will not let him know that until later though. I explain to him that we will need blood and urine specimens and that I'd appreciate it if he cooperates fully. I order him some dinner.

We get an EMS report that they are running code with a 41 year old male with no medical history who had complained of chest pain earlier in the day and collapsed while on vacation with his wife and children. They were on the lake and had just parked their boat at the dock. We perform CPR on him. We shock him several times. We give all the necessary medications, but he does not live. His name is Hank. Hank's wife is beautiful. She was in the room with us, watching, and she told us when to stop CPR. She held it together like a hero. She did better than I could have done in her situation, and I see this every day. It is 4:17pm.

My next patient is a five-year-old boy who tells a good story for an appendicitis. He is much better behaved than our 24-year-old Mr. Donahue. His name is Evan, and he likes the Transformers. I ask him if he's tough like Optimus Prime. He answers with a puny, unexcited, "yeah". I tell Evan that he'll have to have an IV so that we can check his blood and give him medicine if we need to. Evan reluctantly agrees to allow us to give him an IV, but he'll have to wait. His nurse is in another patient's room dealing with a trauma. A 37 year old male was in a motor vehicle accident and was an unrestrained driver. He has obvious facial bruising and neck pain. They're pretty sure he's been drinking.

The radiologist is on the phone. He needs someone to take his report on the chest CT reading for room 5.

Me: "Hey Dr. Paul. It's Marlee."

Dr. Paul (in his thick French accent): "Hey, Marlee. I have uh...Mr. Reed's chest and abdomen CT here. My goodness. Zis is the worst dissection I've ever seen. Zis is not good, Marlee. Nobody is gon to touch zis".

Me: "Aw man. How far does it dissect?"

Dr. Paul: "Zis ting is from zee aortic arch to his femoral, Marlee. Zis is terminal."

Me: "Well thank you for letting us know, Dr. Paul. I'm going to go prepare his family."

Dr. Paul: "How old is zis man?"

Me: "Looks like he's 91, but apparently he's been up traveling, dancing, and was as sharp as a tack until today".

Dr. Paul: "Oh. Tragic. Yes. Definitely. No one will touch zis. OK, thank you, Marlee."

I hang up with Dr. Paul and find my doc to let him know about the reading.

Me: "Room 5 has a dissection from the aortic arch down to the femoral. Dr. Paul said it's the worst one he's ever seen. He says no one will touch it."

Dr. Benson: "Shit. They're such a nice family, man. I knew it."

Me: "Want me to go with you to tell them?"

Dr. Benson: "Sure."

Dr. Benson proceeds to tell Mr. Reed's wife and son that the lining of Mr. Reed's aorta has detached from the vessel wall and that it is inoperable and not compatible with life. Mrs. Reed fell to her knees with her head in her hands. Her son hurried to try and catch her. At this exact moment, Mr. Donahue burst out of his room, this time waving his hands and shouting, "I'm going to kill every last one of you motherfuckers!" I suppose he was fed up with being held against his will. Mrs. Reed jumped to her feet, afraid. "Geodon! NOW!", I yelled. Mr. Donahue's nurse rushed over with her needle and syringe. "Where is security!?" I questioned. I pulled my stethoscope off of my neck and threw it over toward my chair. Dr. Benson and I each grabbed one of Mr. Donahue's arms and pulled him to the ground. The nurse pulled off the needle cap with her teeth, lifted up Mr. Donahue's gown baring everything, and injected the medication into his thigh. Together, we walked him back over to his room. Two other nurses joined in. Security showed up about ten minutes later when Mr. Donahue was already in his bed snoring.

Dr. Benson finished up with the Reeds, and I picked up another chart. I looked at the complaint and sat down at my desk. Looks like I'll be taking care of the drunk driver with the facial trauma. For the first time in years, I actually sit and pay attention to my surroundings. I look around my ER. I think about what the Reeds must be experiencing. How their chance to mourn for their loved one was ruined by a psychotic man who was nearly naked. How the sounds of little Evan's sobs as he got his first IV were muffled by the sound of Mr. Donahue screaming curse words across the department. How a grown man decided to drink and drive and will now have lifelong injuries and a DUI. I wonder if anyone else was injured as a result, and I wonder what kind of self-loathing this man must be going through to be able to make such terrible decisions. And then I think about how this is just another day at the office for me. How none of this is abnormal here. And how completely comfortable I am right here, right now. This is my home. What kind of completely crazy life does one have to live to be able to feel completely content amongst such utter chaos?

I watch Hank's wife through the tiny opening in the curtain as she kisses his forehead. The tube is still in his throat. I wish we had pulled the tube out for her so she didn't have to remember him that way. She doesn't cry. She holds his hand. I wonder what she must be thinking. I wonder what I would think. Today, this woman will tell her children that their father is no longer here. He will not be at their high school graduations. He will not walk them down the aisle on their wedding days. There will be no more fishing trips. They will think of him every day for the rest of their lives. Hank's wife will plan a funeral and bury her husband over the next three days. Shortly after, before she is ready, she will be expected to move on. She sits there looking at her recently deceased husband appearing more stone-faced than me. She won't cry, so I cry for her. I shed four tears, and that is all I allow myself. I am expected to move on too. I clear my throat, blink hard a few times, and wipe my face. It is 4:47pm, and there are five more charts in the rack. Room 3 has an emergency toothache that is a 10/10 on the pain scale.

"As far back as I can remember, I always wanted to be a gangster."

-Ray Liotta as Henry Hill in *Goodfellas*

The Disastrous Conception

One steamy summer night, a man and a woman, who were not in love (in fact, they'd just met earlier in the day), decided to fornicate to the tune of Heart's *All I Want to do is Make Love to You* in the backseat of a beat-up station wagon. I imagine that's how it happened, anyway. This is partly because I believe my parents were super sleazy like that. But it's mostly because my mother actually told me that's how it went down. I don't know why she decided it was appropriate to give me exact details about that fateful evening.

Mom: "We had hung out all day. We were really attracted to each other. Things started getting hot and heavy" (Yes. She actually said that), "and he said 'I don't have a condom'. And I said, 'Well neither do I. It's OK. I love all my kids'".

This was my mother's attempt to strategically describe things to me so I wouldn't think she was a slut. "I love all my kids". This type of exaggerating her love for us so that she could justify her crappy decision-making skills would happen many other times throughout my life. I'd like to think that my mom was thinking about her children that night. But if that were true, we all know she wouldn't have been in that car in the first place. I'm not mad, though. After all, it's how I got here!

Fast forward 9 months. Boom! March 19th, 1985 at Magee Women's Hospital in Pittsburgh, Pennsylvania, I make my debut!

Marcina: "Oh. My. God! It's a GIRL!!!"

I guess she was super excited about this because throughout the pregnancy, they'd thought I was a boy. My mom had already had 3 boys. She thought I was just going to be more of the same - whipping out my little wiener and peeing in plants, telling fart jokes, ruining my school clothes, and never taking a shower. Boy I fooled them! I was going to be named Mark. I feel like that is a boring name, but it would have been OK, I guess. Anyway, the reason for this misunderstanding about my sex was because I have been a deceptive little shit since I was in the womb. Apparently, I had my finger down under my ass on my ultrasound, and they thought it was my little penis. I'd like to think it was my middle finger because that's how I would have chosen to pose in my first-ever portrait.

Now the pressure was on. My mom had to come up with a girl name. I suppose that was exhausting because I only got a first name, Marlee, which is an awesome name. I've never asked my mom why she didn't give me a middle name. I'm sure she'd say something like "oh because we wanted you to be trendy" or "because we wanted it to be cool like 'Madonna'". These would have been bullshit reasons, so I just never asked. So, throughout my life, I've had to explain to people that I don't have a middle name. About half of the people think it's "cool" and "less of a hassle" – yeah, sure. And the other half look at me with these eyes like "oh you poor thing. Your mother didn't love you".

Side note: Over the years, my mom would play that song the whole way through every fucking time it was on the radio. She never reminded me that it was playing the night I was conceived, but I remember it creeping me out every time I heard it. I later downloaded it on my iPod. I still can't listen to it. Waste of $1.99. Also, I actually attended a Heart concert a few years ago because I love Heart. I literally prayed to God that they wouldn't play that song in their set. He answered my prayers. God is such a fucking G.

"Don't pay attention to what they write about you. Just measure it in inches."

-Andy Warhol

The Yinzer Effect

If you are from Pittsburgh, Pennsylvania, you can skip this chapter. Just kidding! Keep reading! There is some good shit in here. You may learn something. I call this chapter "The Yinzer Effect". For those of you not from our freezing cold, smog-covered city, its inhabitants have created its own language, *Pittsburghese*. It is complete with such words as *dahntahn*: down town, as in the main center of commerce within the city. *N'at*: and that. *Worshintin*: Washington, as in Washington, D.C., our nation's capital. *Mahnt Worshintin*: Mount Washington, a place in Pittsburgh with a pretty view, expensive restaurants, and no fucking parking, ever. Oh, and a really kick-ass church. My godson was baptized in this church. *The Picksburgh Stillers*: The best fucking football team in the NFL! These are just a few examples. I shall use some of them in a typical sentence.

"Yinz wanna go dahntahn 'n git a Primanti's sammich n'at? Or yinz just wanna go up Mahnt Worshintin 'n git on the incline"?

Notice the "yinz". "Yinz" is the Pittsburgher's way of saying "you guys", "y'all". And in the really back-country parts of Pittsburgh (Yes. Pittsburgh city limits reach 58.3 square miles. There are some country parts of Pittsburgh), it's pronounced "yunce" or "younz".

I use "yinzer effect" in an effort to describe the expectations placed on us when we are born in Pittsburgh or are just the product of two Pittsburgh natives who have since moved elsewhere and procreated. There are certain rules that one must adhere to if she is going to survive in this city.

Rule #1: You will LOVE the Pittsburgh Steelers.

You will bleed black and gold. Your first hat will be a Pittsburgh Steelers hat. Your hospital pictures will be taken with you wearing said hat. You will also be wearing a Steelers onesie. If you're a girl, said hat and onesie may be pink, but this is absolutely not necessary. Your booties will also be black and gold. And you will have at least 3 Steelers outfits at any given time at any point in your life until you die. You will be required to watch every Steelers game until you die regardless of whether you move to Florida or Alabama or Montana or some other bullshit state where they don't broadcast the Steelers game unless you're at a shitty bar. And if there is a Steelers bar in that state, you will go to that bar to watch the game because if you go to any other bar, there is a chance that people will be Ravens or Browns fans, and your ass will inevitably go to jail that day, and it's just not worth it. Find the Steelers bar.

Rule #2: You will consequently also LOVE the Pittsburgh Pirates, the Pittsburgh Penguins, the Pitt Panthers (especially during March Madness), and occasionally the Penn State Nittany Lions. You will somehow manage to argue that Mario Lemieux and Jaromir Jagr are better hockey players than Wayne Gretzky, even though you know you're bullshitting. You will understand that Roberto Clemente was more important to the great American pastime than Babe Ruth. You will also own a Mario Lemieux, Jaromir Jagr, and an Andrew McCutchen jersey for the days in which you are not wearing your Steelers jerseys.

Rule #3: You will LOVE Primanti Brothers a.k.a. Primanti's. "What is Primanti's", you ask? It is a famous restaurant which serves sandwiches that include a meat of your choice with coleslaw, french fries, provolone cheese, and a tomato stacked high and stuffed between two pieces of Mancini's bread. Get the Pitts-burger. Some people opt to have a fried egg thrown there. That scares me. A Primanti's sandwich is like crack. I guess that would still be like crack with a fried egg, so I could see how some people may like that. Also pertaining to this rule is the rule that if you're a girl in Pittsburgh, you will share your Primanti's sandwich with your best girlfriend so you don't look like a total fat ass. Don't worry though. You can totally substitute your lack of half a sandwich with a side of fries, but only if you also order these fries with a side of cheese. Or two. Two sides of cheese is totally acceptable. Also if you're a guy taking a girl on a date to Primanti's, order her some fries with cheese. Bitches in Pittsburgh will straight up marry a dude who orders her fries with cheese. At the very least, you'll get a blow job. This also applies to Kennywood's Potato Patch fries and cheese. As a Pittsburgh chick, you will search the world for fries and cheese, but you will never find any as good as these. Trust me.

Rule #4: You will also LOVE Mancini's bread so that you can go enjoy yourself a Primanti's sandwich and any other sandwich you ever make in your Pittsburgh-living life.

Rule #5: Pizza with ranch = a meal. Pizza without ranch = shit, even if it does come from Fiori's. Or Beto's. Put the ranch on the pizza. Or dip it. Just have the ranch available at all times.

Rule #6: You will frequent Gus and Yai Yai's in West Park for an iceball. You will sit far enough away from the homeless folks to not be intimidated but close enough to eavesdrop on them. You will feed the pigeons popcorn, but you will not sacrifice any iceball sweetness for those dirty damn birds. You will also go to West Park or Riverview Park to drive around and smoke blunts...if you're into that sort of thing and if you're still in high school. If you're out of high school, and you're still driving around in Riverview Park smoking blunts, get your shit together. Seriously!

Rule #7: Regardless of your school rivalry, you will still come together to "rep" the 412. 412 is Pittsburgh's area code. There is now a 724 area code for some of Pittsburgh, but that doesn't count. I've known people who actually have a cell phone with a 724 area code who have a "412" tattoo. I get it.

Rule #8: The rich history of the city of Pittsburgh is more important than the history of any other part of this country or of this world. It's the most important history one can learn! From steel mills to Sarah Heinz house to finally blowing up the Civic Arena. From the submarine that sits outside the Carnegie Science Center to the art in The Andy Warhol Museum. Know it, all of it. And be proud of where you came from!

Rule #9: You will grow up Catholic and then inevitably question the *shit* out of this religion after you experience all the crazy things this city has to offer.

Rule #10: You will be forced to be tough as nails. As a woman, you will be unrefined and totally rough-around-the-edges. You will carry this with you for the rest of your life, even if you try to move away. Even if the place you move to is Alabama. They will try to make you a southern belle, but all you will end up with is a fake accent (mixed with your yinzer-isms) and a few extra pounds from fried okra and Popeye's Chicken.

You will know how to fight, and I don't mean argue, although we're good at that, too. I mean fist fight. Come on! You grew up wearing cut-off Steelers jerseys with unzipped daisy duke shorts and heels! You smoked cigarettes at age fourteen and weed a few months later! Your first drink was either a shot of Jameson given to you by your uncle at a St. Patty's Day party when you were twelve, or better yet, a sip of wine from the communion cup at age eight – it was the perk to putting in all that work to make your First Holy

Communion. We actually have to study for that shit. Your parents encouraged your first underage drink. They supplied the alcohol for your house parties. And all the kids in your class came to your high school graduation party to get lit because your parents supplied it, and their parents were also coming to the party. Nobody cared if you were drinking. Plus they were paying for it! You got your belly button pierced at fourteen, nose pierced at fifteen, tongue pierced at sixteen, and your first tattoo by seventeen. You were at Club Zoo the night you got your belly button pierced, showing it off and dry humping eighteen year old dudes. You couldn't go to Jets, which was a way better club, because your parents were NOT going to drive your ass all the way out to Harmarville for you to be a little slut! Especially because the only way to get there was to drive on highway 28. Fuck. That.

But you were tough. Because you learned how to socialize with people who were older than you. And you learned how to lie to adults, mainly about your actual age so you could get in to the club. And you had to stand up to those older bitches who wanted to dance on the big speaker. You had to tell them to move over and let your younger, hotter ass up there! You just spent $25 of your allowance at Charlotte Russe on that shirt, and you were going to fucking show it off! And in case those girls decided to get in your face, you had to know how to intimidate them right back. And that bitch was usually also a fellow Pittsburgh girl. So she'd either push you or throw a punch. And you had to anticipate that and be able to push harder or throw a better punch. Because this is Pittsburgh, and girls will fight. Also girls in Pittsburgh will fight dudes...without batting an overly-mascaraed eyelash. Because if a Pittsburgh bitch is in the mood to fight, she doesn't care if you're a guy. She will scream in your face and then punch you in it. Take my best friend, Tarah, for example. Tarah is 5'2". 120 lbs. Tiny person. Big mouth! Every time we go out, Tarah manages to want to fight a dude. Or pull her pants down right in the middle of the street to take a piss. Or just piss right in her pants and then sit right on that chair in Tom's Diner with her pissed-in pants and have her

17

some eggs and bacon. Because Tarah is a classic Pittsburgh girl. And we don't give a fuck. Pittsburgh girls are some of the most gorgeous girls in the world. We know how to doll ourselves up and put on a show. But we're tough! Like a mix between Jersey Shore and inner-city New York. We're the worst!

"I'm completely in favor of the separation of Church and State. These two institutions screw us up enough on their own, so both of them together is certain death.

-George Carlin

Peace Be with You

After my birth, my mom took me home to our house on a hill in Bellevue, PA. Bellevue is a suburb of Pittsburgh. It's about twelve minutes from *dahntahn*. Twenty-eight stairs to get to the front door of that motherfucker, and I still managed to be a fat kid for most of my childhood. You can see the Steel Building from my attic window. I don't give a shit what they call the Steel Building now. When I was there, that's what it was called. Anyway, my earliest childhood memory involves me and my little sister Rachel repetitively running across the living room and jumping on the couch at my dad's house. Don't ask me why my mom and my dad had separate houses then. I guess they were destined not to make it at that whole marriage thing. My dad was a super nice guy, apparently really mellow. But I guess we managed to piss him off that day. He warned us to stop jumping on the couch about thirty times before he finally decided to come over a lightly tap us on the ass in an attempt to discipline us. Part of me was pissed at him because it was my first (of many) spankings, but the other part of me was proud of him. I had always taken him for a pushover prior to that.

Some of my other earliest childhood memories took place at my dad's house. He lived on the South Side Slopes. So, basically it was a row of houses stacked right on top of each other that are all ready to slide right off the side of the fucking hill if it rains in Pittsburgh one more time. My grandfather owned a cleaning and restoration business right down the street from there. My dad worked for him. They cleaned the skyscrapers and tunnels *n'at*. My grandfather was a big deal. He was a good businessman. He was also a phenomenal mobster. No shit. I'm pretty sure my grandfather was "connected". There were twenty men wearing black suits and dark sunglasses at his funeral, men none of us had ever seen before. I hope mafia men don't read autobiographies written by nobody 32-year-old women. I don't want to die that way. Anyway I liked going to my dad's office because the secretary, Jo Ann, gave me food and candy all the time.

My dad's house was boring, though. I remember discovering clover mites while sitting on the sidewalk one day. They're little red bugs that look like ticks. Gross little things. I used to smear them across the ground and make "paintings". Things were obviously really eventful at my dad's. I also remember that my dad had a pet tarantula and that my dad's cousin Jimmy accidentally stepped on that tarantula one day after getting super high on heroin. My dad was also a participant in such behavior. Shooting heroin, not tramping on tarantulas. My dad died from liver failure when I was four years old. His name was Denis. My later medical experience would teach me that he had hepatitis C from IV drug abuse, and it ultimately killed him. Everybody tells me he was really nice.

Except for these few things you've read here, I don't remember anything about him. I've seen pictures of him holding my little sister and me. He seemed to really care about us. He was a biker dude, which I think is awesome! He was a badass. Later discussions with my drunken older brothers would lead to my discovering that one night, he was involved in a drug-deal gone badly. Apparently I was also involved in this drug deal. I was a baby in the car with him when the shit went down. Somehow he managed to get away and save me. I'm not mad that he would take me on a drug deal. People on heroin are obviously not excellent decision-makers.

I remember the funeral. I also remember that the point of that funeral was to mourn the loss of my father, but I was way more concerned about getting my older cousin to play patty cake with me. I was a real pain in the ass about it. But I got my way because everybody felt bad for Rachel, my kid sister, and me. I remember we both held hands and walked up to the little kneeling bench in front of the casket together. We knelt down and started to pray because we were told to. I didn't understand that I was supposed to pray for the salvation of my deceased father's soul so that he wouldn't sit in Purgatory for all eternity, so I just prayed for a new bike. I never asked Rachel what she prayed for. I remember looking around when we were done, and everyone in the room was staring at us and crying. I remember wondering what the fuck was wrong with them. Now that I've been to countless funerals, I get it.

One day, after falling in love with another man, my mother packed us up and moved us to "the mountains". She was going to marry this guy. This would be her fifth marriage. She still owned the big, beautiful house in Pittsburgh, but she moved us to a tiny shack in Somerset County, Pennsylvania – essentially the middle of nowhere. This area has since gained a little fame because it is where one of the planes crashed on September 11th, so now it is "famous" for being "that place in the middle of nowhere where one of the 9/11 planes crashed". I don't remember anything about that place except my brother Jason had an ATV, and he always got in trouble with it. The boys also had a treehouse that I was not granted access to because I was a girl, so I just snuck up in that bitch every day while they were at school. Suck it.

This new stepdad was a real winner. I remember one night, he forced Rachel and me to stay up late and watch a super scary movie. I found that really odd, even at the time. That stuff was NOT for kids. I thought he was a creeper. It turns out he really was because he apparently repetitively sexually molested Rachel for a few years. I knew nothing about it until I was an adult. If I had known, I would have poisoned that son of a bitch. My mom ultimately divorced him, and we moved back to Pittsburgh. He later died a lonely man. I only know this because they had to contact my mother to inform her of his death since apparently they had no other contacts. She told them to do whatever they wanted with his remains and that she wanted nothing to do with it. He deserved it.

Thank God we got to come back home! It was time for me to start kindergarten. My mom enrolled my brother Corey and me in catholic school. Corey was 5 years older than me. He was NOT cool with the idea of going to the same school as his little sisters. He was responsible for walking us to school every day when my mom couldn't drive us, which was pretty much every day. He hated this responsibility. One day he proved it by running into our room yelling "Girls! Hurry up! You slept in! You're late for school!" Rachel and I spring out of bed and put on our sweet-ass school uniforms, brush our teeth and hair, and go to find Corey. He was in his bed, sleeping. "Cor! We're ready! Let's go! We gotta go!" He laughed and laughed and said, "You idiots! It's 3 a.m. Go back to bed!" Son of a bitch! He tricked us! We were 5 and 6 years old. At least once a week, he'd run away from us on the way home from school and tell us he was leaving us in the street. We'd try to keep up, but we couldn't. We'd stand in the middle of the street and cry and think we were stranded forever. And he'd pop out from behind a tree and say, "Come on, yinz jagoffs". He really did love us.

My mother was a devout catholic. I'm talking McDonald's Filet-O-Fish every Friday during Lent kind of devout! We did not eat meat on Fridays during Lent. We had to give something up for Lent every year. We had to kneel by our beds and say our prayers every night. We prayed for all the poor souls who were stuck in Purgatory to get into Heaven. We sang hymns. We went to catholic school and walked around with black shit on our foreheads every Ash Wednesday. But we did not step foot inside the church unless it was Thursday morning at 0800 and mandatory for school. And inevitably, Thursdays were the only days my mom could drive us to school. She was obviously really concerned about us getting to church on time because we were late every single week. Corey would get to the front door and run in and tell us to wait at least a minute to come in because he didn't want anyone to know we "belonged" to him. So I would wait one minute and grab Rachel's hand, dip it in the holy water, make the sign of the cross on her, then on myself, hang my head low, and find a seat in the back of the church with the townspeople. I was too embarrassed to go through the trouble of finding our classes so we could sit with them. Plus, it had happened so often that our teachers just expected to find us in the back once the service was over. I remember finally telling my mom it embarrassed me to get to church late every week. "I'm doing the best I can do! I'm trying to be the mother and the father! Trying to work and make sure you kids have a roof over your head!" Eventually I stopped trying to convince her to get us there on time. I still don't know the Nicene Creed because I always missed the beginning of the service. So now I just mouth "watermelon" while they say it. Forgive me, Father.

I later found out that since the death of my father, my mother collected a good chunk of change monthly from social security for my sister and me. I knew nothing of it until I was an adult. She says she spent it to "keep a roof over" my head. All the number of times I'd heard that made me wish I'd lived in a cardboard box.

While we're on the subject of church, I'd like to describe a few of my experiences making the holy sacraments. I don't remember my baptism because I was a baby. I made my First Reconciliation when I was seven. As a Catholic, your First Reconciliation is the first time you ever go into the confessional booth and tell the priest all the sins you've committed. At age seven. Things like "I fed the dog a piece of my pizza even though my mom said I wasn't allowed" and "I called my little sister a bitch because she deserved it". I was a more mature seven-year-old than most, so I'd already

23

learned what a bitch was, and sometimes Rachel really was a bitch! My sister and I were able to make our First Reconciliation at the same time, so my mom found it fitting that she should also participate in confession that day. We all went to the church together, along with all the other kids in my class and their parents. My mom let Rachel and me go into the booth first. I picked Father Paul because he was young (and handsome). And I figured he'd understand me. Plus I initially thought to ask him for his number, but I figured that wouldn't work out after I'd confessed that I was sorry for thinking Father Paul was handsome. I was probably in there for three minutes. He made me say five Hail Marys, and I was cleansed of my sins from seven whole years. I think that's a pretty good deal.

Next was my mom's turn to go in. I imagine it went something like this, "Forgive me, Father. For I have sinned. It has been forty-seven years since my last confession". That's an exaggeration, but it had definitely been a long time since her last confession because that bitch was in there for five fucking hours! But I was seven at the time, so it was probably more like a half hour, which is still excessively long. I remember being nervous that all my classmates would know my mom was a sinner because they had to leave Father Paul's line to go confess to Father Dennis. And then they would all be pissed at me because Father Dennis was mean and scary. My mom finally emerged from the confessional booth, sobbing, with black mascara dripping down her face. She told us that she felt so much better and thanked us for making our First Reconciliation. I was done with my Hail Marys within two minutes. I spent the rest of the time convincing Rachel to play pretend trench warfare with me and lay in the pew as still and quiet as possible, hoping no one would see us waiting for our mother. My mom spent ten minutes on her Hail Marys and ultimately decided she could finish them at home. I wonder how many she had to say.

About a year after that, we made our First Holy Communion. That's where you get the little wafer and wine, and it nourishes your body with the body and blood of Jesus Christ. I was really excited about this. I knew it was a big deal in Catholicism, and this would also be my first drink of wine. My mom invited everyone she knew to come and celebrate that day with us, including my big brothers. Everyone but my brother Barry went up to receive communion together. Jason went up and got himself a wafer and booze, and he's not even Catholic. He was just following the crowd. I guess my mom was not so into religion when she was raising Barry. Barry is old enough to be my father. My mom was sixteen when she had him, so I don't think religion was a priority in his young life.

I cupped my hands, walked up to the priest, he said, "The body of Christ. Amen," to which I replied, "Amen". I ate the wafer. It tasted like shit. I walked over to the lady who was holding the cup of wine. We also exchanged Amens. I took the cup and forcefully raised it to my mouth, accidentally splashing a little bit on my chin. I wasn't expecting the cup to be that full! I remember my mother telling me a story about a man accidentally dropping his blessed wafer on the ground. He ate it anyway. He felt so ashamed for dropping a piece of Jesus on the ground, he knelt down on the floor and started kissing the ground where the wafer had fallen. And here I was with the Blood of Christ dripping from my face. I had a mini panic attack because I didn't want to be seen wiping the blood of Christ off my face like a drunken sailor, so I just obnoxiously stuck my tongue out to lap it up. It was then that I decided that wine was also gross. That was the first and only time I've ever drunk the Blood of Christ. Not because I'm against it. Just because I don't like wine. And, also, because I will forever be fearful of being an adult having to figure out how to get dripping, blessed wine off my face without anyone noticing.

I returned to the aisle just in time to hear Barry saying, "Fucking Catholics! Stand. Sit. Kneel. Sit. Stand. Kneel. Let all these fucking people walk past you while you're trying to kneel. What the fuck is wrong with you people!?" I remember thinking Barry should have been struck by lightning at that very moment. Or at least he should have had to say twenty Hail Marys for using obscenities in church. Neither of these things happened. Barry would later go on to convert to Eastern Orthodox Catholicism so that he could marry his beautiful wife in her own church. You think Roman Catholic services are crazy? Go to a Greek Orthodox mass. I don't blame him for ultimately being a hypocrite, though. My sister-in-law is the shit.

"I'm a hustler, baby. I just want you to know."

-Pharrell Williams

The Early Entrepreneurial Years

Perhaps the worst mistake our Catholic school administration ever made was trusting a seven- and eight-year-old kid from the hood with no parental guidance to sell candy bars for a fundraiser. I don't remember much about the seminar, but I do remember someone offering Rachel and me as many boxes of chocolate bars as we thought we could sell. I also remember something about possibly winning a lava lamp and a T shirt if we sold a certain number of them.

So, I asked, "How many do we gotta sell to get the lava lamp?"

Candy lady: "150 candy bars".

Me: "How much does each candy bar sell for?"

Candy lady: "$1.00".

Me: "Done!"

I took 150 candy bars, and Rachel and I immediately started selling. We walked home from school that day. By that point, we didn't need Corey anymore. We knew our way. We sold all 150 candy bars by the time we got home. We stashed the money in my top drawer. As soon as I got to school the next day, I asked for 100 more candy bars. They gave them to me without hesitation. Since we only hit-up the same houses we'd just sold to the day before, we were only able to sell 50 candy bars that day. I thought that was still pretty good. When we got home, we threw the leftover candy bars on the bed and grabbed the $150 from the drawer. We now had $200 and 50 candy bars in total. Plus, we were well on our way to a new hot pink lava lamp and a new Nickelodeon shirt. We were going shopping! The corner store was about two blocks from our house, shorter if we took the alley. It was light outside, so we opted for the alley. A seven- and an eight-year-old. Walking down the alley. With $200 cash. It sounds like we're going to get robbed, but that's not what this story is about. This story is about entrepreneurs. Plus, Rachel was well on her way to having a red belt in Tae Kwon Do by this point. No one was going to be robbing us. We spent all $200 in the corner store. We bought pop, candy cigarettes, more candy bars (don't ask me why), chips, magazines, whatever we wanted. I'm pretty sure you can buy a whole store like that for $200. And the cashier didn't seem at all suspicious. So we made our way home with all of our loot. We ate half of the stuff on the way. My mom was laying on the couch when we got home. She asked us what we were doing. See...it was a regular thing for Rachel and me to be out running the streets at that age. She just wanted to know what all the plastic bags stuffed with convenience store shit were about. We proceeded to tell her that the school had given us these free candy bars and offered to give us other free stuff if we just sold them, so we sold all but 50 of them. Then, we spent the money we made at the corner store, and we couldn't wait to tell the candy lady that we'd sold almost all of our candy bars so that we could get our lava lamp and T shirt.

My mom was fucking furious! Apparently, we'd missed the point that we were supposed to sell candy bars for the school and then return the money to the school. We weren't supposed to be making shit! Suddenly the stupid lava lamp and the T shirt weren't so cool. My mom grabbed the spatula and ran at me to whoop my ass. Rachel jumped in front of the spatula shouting "Take me instead!" and took the beating for me. This would happen several more times throughout our lives. I would get Rachel involved in some shit, my mom would go to beat me, and Rachel would take the bullet. If ever there was a time when Rachel was due to receive the beating, I'd be outside, down all 28 stairs, and half way down the block on my big wheel before my mom could even get back with that spatula! I'm sorry for that, Rachel.

My mom was stuck paying back the $200 and had to take the remaining 50 candy bars to work to sell them, which was bullshit because I found wrappers for those candy bars all over the house. I bet she kept about twenty of them. I believe that when I have children, I will never allow them to sell candy bars (or anything else) for fundraisers. Lava lamps and T shirts are just not worth it. There was only one other time when I took the plunge and sold candy bars as a fundraiser. I was in 7th grade on the basketball team and couldn't afford the shoes we were required to buy. I attempted to sell the candy bars, but what ultimately happened was that two of the older girls on my team stole and ate almost all of them during one of our games. Bitches. It's OK though, because Corey ended up dating one of them later and totally broke her heart. He cheated on her with her best friend or something scandalous like that. And the other one was a rather mannish lady who ended up in jail. Revenge!

I had other entrepreneurial endeavors as a youngster. I learned early-on that I was going to have to be a hustler to get by. When I was fourteen, I dated a guy who was a total pothead. We'll talk more about him later. He's important in this chapter because he always had weed around. Sometimes he attempted to sell it, but he was terrible at dealing drugs. He didn't have a steady clientele, he smoked up more than half of his stash, and he slept most of the day, so no one could ever get ahold of him. I decided to take over his business. I didn't smoke weed. I had only smoked it for about two weeks when I initially started dating him then never touched it again. I never liked it, but it was a good way to make some money, so I started giving everyone my phone number rather than his so they could get ahold of me during the day. I already knew the main supplier, so I started harmlessly flirting with him to get a better deal. I made a lot of money for a fourteen year old kid. This went on for a few months until I decided it probably wasn't a good way to make a living. Who would have thought that eighteen years later, I'd still be in the business of dealing drugs?

Once I decided I could no longer live the hard-knock life of an adolescent drug dealer, I started searching for other ways to make money. I needed something less risky. It turns out that Rachel had been running her own business for several months, too. I decided to go in on it with her. Rachel's plan was to ride the PAT bus from our house in Bellevue over to West View (the next town over) to K-Mart. Once there, she would load up a buggy with cartons of cigarettes and roll it right out of the store without anyone noticing. Then her and her crew would shove the cigarettes in their baggy clothes, get back on the bus, and return home to distribute the cigarettes. I was allowed in when Rachel realized that she had poor spending habits and could no longer afford bus fare for her and her posse. I supplied the dough for the bus ride and helped sell the cigarettes, so I got a cut. These shenanigans went on for *way* longer than they should have. Finally one day, Rachel got caught, and the K-Mart security officer called my house. Luckily, we had caller ID, and luckily, I was home that day and my mom wasn't. But that security officer thought he had a whole conversation with my mother that day, complete with how bad I was going to whoop her ass when she got home and how many Hail Marys she was going to have to say. I pleaded with him to please let her return home on the bus because I had let a family member borrow my car that day, so I couldn't come and get her. He agreed, and Rachel showed up grinning from ear to ear within about 30 minutes. You see, Rachel was a 13-year-old kid at the time. She was short and petite and looked like she was about eight. She had bleach blonde hair and piercing blue eyes. And she always put on a good show. She was the perfect partner in crime – a cunning little con-artist, just like me. Neither of us

30

were upset that our operation was over because we knew the glory days had lasted much longer we had anticipated. My mother never found out about that incident, or that business, because Rachel and me were tight like that. And we had to do what we had to do to eat.

"She was never crazy. She just didn't let her heart settle in a cage. She was born wild, and sometimes we need people like her. For it's the horrors in her heart which cause the flames in ours. And she was always willing to burn for everything she has ever loved."

-R.M. Drake

Marcina

Have you ever met a person and thought, "You're more like a cartoon character than a real human being"? Someone who is just so bizarre that you think maybe they're make-believe? Marcina Louise Scacchi Wingard DuMont Meenan Bruno Harr Ensley Dillinger. That's a mouthful, isn't it? Scacchi was my mom's maiden name. She was of Italian and Cherokee Indian descent. Her father, my Pappy Joe, was an Italian man who proudly referred to himself as the "Dago on the West Side Hill". He worked in a coal mine all his life. He had coke-bottle glasses and rosacea, which had caused his nose to grow twice the size of a normal man's. He was a pervy guy, never to me, but I remember him always flirting with 18-year-old waitresses at restaurants and saying things like, "Sweetie, come over here and put your finger in my coffee. It needs more sugar". Gross. My Pappy Joe was famous for making surprise visits to our house with a bucket of KFC chicken so he could "check up on things". I remember it had been a while since the last time I'd seen him, and he told me to come sit on his lap, like he always did. I had put on a few pounds since the last time. "JESUS CHRIST! Marcina what the HELL are you feeding these kids!?" The answer was nothing. My mother rarely fed us, but I supplied my body with nourishment from school lunches (when she remembered to actually give me lunch money, which was rarely) and snacks from the corner store I mentioned earlier. It didn't bother me that my grandfather had just called me a fat ass. I was more concerned with getting my hands on a piece of that fried chicken. Then he would sing to me, the song he always sang to me.

"There goes Marlee floatin' down the Delaware.
Chewin' on her underwear.
Couldn't afford another pair.
Ten days later, bitten by a polar bear.
Poor old polar bear died."

My Pappy Joe was a dick. No one in my family will argue that. He had one friend, Tony, another equally miserable old man. He did some decent things, though, like the KFC and ice cream cones. And he made us little reindeer and jewelry boxes from wood. He was an extremely talented woodworker, and he ultimately took over payments on my saxophone when my mom threatened to stop paying for it because it was too expensive. She later sold it without asking my permission when I was away at college.

Pappy Joe hated my mom. He brought us food because he knew we were being neglected. There wasn't a single time he came to visit that he and my mother weren't involved in a brutal argument. I remember one Thanksgiving, there was such a battle between them that ultimately the only people left at the table were Rachel and me. And that was only because we finally had some fucking food on the table, and we were not missing that for the world. In fact, most Thanksgivings ended up in chaos like that in my household. It was expected. It was normal for us.

My grandmother's name was Marge. I have only spoken to her once since I was ten. The one time I did see her, I was in town visiting during undergrad, and my nephew was going to visit her. My nephew had maintained contact with her over the years. We sat down on her couch, and she looked at me. She said, "Erik, your new girlfriend sure is pretty". I said, "I'm Marlee, gram". I guess I had expected her to have some kind of dramatic reaction. I expected her to be happy to finally see me. I felt like she should have a lot to tell me, to teach me. Because she was my grandmother. And it wasn't my fault I didn't get to see her. "Oh", she said. And went on knitting. My mother had forbidden us from speaking with her when we were very young. I don't know the reason for this, but I do know that later in my life, around high school, my *Papa* Fred (grandma's 2nd husband) became my *uncle* Fred and started living in our house with us and sleeping in the same bed as my mom. My mom referred to every new main-squeeze as *uncle*, and she thought we believed her. The concept of Uncle Fred didn't last long, maybe about 3 months. I came home from school one day, and he was gone. I never asked where he went because that was a fucked-up situation, and I didn't give two shits about Uncle Papa Fred.

My grandmother was a mean old lady who never liked anyone. She had ridiculously high expectations for everyone she ever came across, so inevitably everyone was a disappointment. When I was about eight, my aunt Fuzzy would take Rachel and me over to see her. I don't remember anything else about my grandmother except that she made the best buttered toast on Italian bread and hot chocolate. My grandma Marge was my last surviving grandparent, and she died at the age of 83 a few months ago. I didn't go to her funeral.

Now that you know where my mother came from, you may be able to understand her. No, you won't. I've spent my whole life trying. I have heard stories from my mother's childhood, but of course she was always the narrator, and life has taught me not to believe a thing my mother says. But I do think she had it rough. Apparently neither of my grandparents cared for her at any point in her life. She said she only had one dress when she was a kid. That was her only piece of clothing. By high school, she had two outfits. Her parents never drove her to school, never asked her how she was doing in school, never attended one PTA meeting. Not one play. Never helped with a single homework assignment. She had one friend growing up. When my mom turned sixteen, she decided that she would get pregnant so that she could be emancipated from her home. She married my oldest brother's father when she was seventeen. She moved out and began her life as a wife and mother. I don't know what happened with that marriage, but it didn't last long. I later met this man when he came to my house to visit repetitively in the evenings. He slept over too. He was a nice man. He died a few years ago. I can't remember what took him.

Marcina was a single mother with an infant, who had relied heavily on her now ex-husband, was emancipated at age 16, and therefore did not achieve her high school diploma. She said she had nowhere to go, so she applied for government assistance. She said this allowed her to get some food stamps so that she could feed herself and my big brother. In exchange for this, though, she had to work in a daycare in the basement of a church. She said it was miserable and hot, and the food stamps just weren't worth it. So after two weeks in that church basement, she moved to Pittsburgh, Pennsylvania with her baby to get her GED. Shortly after obtaining her GED, she started nursing school. She fell in love again, got married, and gave birth to my big brother Jason. I've only ever heard stories about Jason's father. The last story I heard was that he was seen standing on a wooden box in downtown Pittsburgh claiming to be the Son of God. He thought he was the Messiah. My mom must have thought he was a douche because she left him. He also died a few years ago. I suppose it was from complications of being a fucking lunatic.

My mom really enjoyed her nursing career. It was something she truly loved. And she loved my big brothers, so much so that she decided to give me another one, Corey Ward Meenan. My mom married Corey's dad because she was completely infatuated with him. She said he showed her the time of her life. He was a big spender, and he was terribly charming. He bought her a beautiful diamond ring. They spent their honeymoon in Aruba. She spent the whole trip begging him to stop drinking, gambling, and snorting cocaine. Corey's father was really into his faith, so it was during this time that my mom had become a devout Catholic. Maybe it was because that was an interest they'd shared together, or maybe it was because she was on her way to a third failed marriage. Either way, she was serious about it. Some of my earliest childhood memories of my mother involve watching video tapes of her being handcuffed and thrown by her long, curly, blonde hair into the back of a police wagon during protests. She hated the idea of abortion, and she did whatever she could to make sure it didn't happen. I don't know why she was so passionate about it, but she was. One time, she let rats loose in an abortion clinic. Another time, she laid fetuses found in the clinic dumpster on the lawn in front of the clinic. At one point, she also convinced some of the Hell's Angels to cause a ruckus outside the building so no one could get in. My mom was drop-dead gorgeous back then. She was also conniving and vindictive. She could have talked a man into licking the bottom of her shoe after she'd stepped in a fresh pile of dog shit.

I guess my mom had to find a passion because things were not so passionate in her relationship with her husband. She ultimately left him and then found my dad. Of all my brothers' fathers, I knew Corey's dad the best. I have memories of all of us staying at his house after my dad died. It was there, at age six, that I saw my first Playboy magazine, neatly placed among the cookbooks in the kitchen. I don't know why my mother found it necessary to always return to her ex-husbands. I tried to maintain a cordial relationship with Corey's father, and I was able to tolerate him pretty well for several years even though he was an ass. You see, this guy thought he was a big deal. He owned a restaurant and made a little more money than my mom was used to. He ultimately lost everything due to several consecutive years of tax evasion. He walked abnormally slowly and talked to everyone like they were inferior. He always reminded me of Paulie from

Goodfellas, except not quite as nice. I felt obligated to maintain a relationship with him because I wanted him to be around for my niece, Hailee, and my nephew, Perry, and I somehow thought I could make sure that would happen. I had to give up on that, though, when I called him very excited that I had passed the physician assistant board exam, and he immediately replied with, "Good! I need you to write me a prescription for some Tussionex". Tussionex is a narcotic cough medication. He wanted me to put my brand new license on the line so that he could feed his addiction. I've only spoken with him once since then, and it was only to tell him to kiss my ass when he demanded that I escort him to the casket during a funeral.

I really didn't like him because he was mean to my brother. I remember one night Corey took us over to his dad's house to babysit us and hang out and play Zelda. We were awakened in the middle of the night when Corey's dad came in drunk, screaming about how Corey forgot to empty the trash. So he showed Corey how to empty the trash by pouring the trash bag out over my brother while he was sleeping in his bed. There was a point later when Corey actually made the choice to go and live with his dad. He didn't get along with my mom's new boyfriend, and he also hated the guy's son. So Corey beat up the son on the playground one day. The kid totally deserved it. I was there. This, in turn, caused my mom's new boyfriend to beat Corey with the metal part of his belt and with his fists. This guy was 6'4", 260lbs. He was a state constable. And he was also a certified piece of shit. I remember Corey sitting there on the bed, bloody, with a broken nose. So stoic. He didn't even cry.

"If you want the ultimate rush, you've got to be willing to pay the ultimate price! It's not tragic to die doing what you love!"
-Patrick Swayze as Bodhi in *Point Break*

Slumdog Debonair

Now I'm about eight years old. My mother was single and ready to mingle, so she started dropping us off at random houses for weeks at a time so that she could go do whatever she had to do. OK not random, but ghetto. There was this lady who worked with my mom. Her name was Tina. Tina must have thought it was time for my mom to find a new piece of ass because she volunteered to watch us regularly. I hated Tina's house. She had two bad little kids, a boy and a girl, and I hated them. I plotted to kill them sometimes, and Rachel was also totally down for this madness. Relax. I never would have done it. Anyway, Tina lived in a house exactly the size of a Playskool playhouse, complete with plastic kitchenware and foods that only had a shelf life of greater than two years. We ate hot dogs and macaroni and cheese every time we went to Tina's house, which was basically six out of seven days. I know I shouldn't be complaining because it was better than what we got at home, but everything tasted like dawn dish detergent. And I don't know how that was because this lady didn't even own dish detergent. But for the sake of not dying, I ate it. And I encouraged Rachel to eat it, too, praying that it didn't contain any remnants of the rat poison that was strategically sprinkled around the tiny house.

We would also sometimes go to Heather's house. Heather was my brother Jason's baby mama. They have three children together, but they never got married, which was probably a good call on both of their behalves. Jason was an

38

ass to Heather, and Heather was too dumb to get out. I remember one time when Jason got drunk (and this happened a lot), he pushed Heather's mother down the stairs. I had front row tickets to that brawl. She lived on the North Side of Pittsburgh, in the middle of the ghetto. Her house was also about to slide off the cliff or cave in from the top. I remember always being afraid to sit on the toilet because the floor was so rotten, I thought I'd fall through, toilet and all.

Heather was the coolest chick in the world. She was pretty, and she cooked like a master chef. She worked at Taco Bell. She played good music and danced around the living room with us like we were her friends. She loved us like we were her little sisters. That was the first time in my life that I'd felt important. Heather spent time with us. She paid attention to us. She wasn't too busy doing other things. She just wanted to hang out with us. I remember one night, after about a week of not seeing my mom, she pulled up outside of Heather's house driving a purple sports car. She was blasting music and yelled for everyone to come check out her new ride. Apparently this was the first of many midlife crises for my mother, so she decided to buy a new purple car. She would later give that shitty little car to Corey who would ultimately sell it for way more than it was worth to the pothead ex-boyfriend I mentioned earlier. She got rid of the purple Probe to buy a gunmetal gray Mustang GT 5.0.

I have so many memories of the Mustang. She played George Thorogood's *Bad to the Bone* on repeat. That car had a customized decal of a topless blonde riding a horse with a nursing degree covering her boobs on the back fender. My mom once threw an ice cream sundae at me in the back seat of that car because I complained about not getting the same shitty Dilly Bar that all the rest of the kids got. She got the sundae special for me. I still feel stupid about that. There was ice cream and strawberry syrup all over the place, and she did not give one single fuck. And I could tell that she would have thrown that thing a thousand times over to see me shut up as fast as I did. I spent three days cleaning that up. I remember driving through a tunnel when my mom noticed a lady half her age drunk driving. She pulled up and rolled down my window and yelled, "Get off the fuckin' ROAD!" I could see my mom struggling with something down by the gas pedal as she was yelling. She took off her shoe, whipped it right past my face, out my window, and into the other lady's window. It smacked her right in her face. The lady pulled over. My mom kept on driving as though nothing happened. She said nothing more about it. My mom could throw a shoe like a boomerang. That was a normal form of punishment in our household. She worked hard, and she didn't want to move from the couch, so she'd pick up her shoe and throw it as hard as she could. It would turn the corner, hit us in the back of the head, and return gently into my mother's hand. Sometimes I find myself practicing this technique. I suck at it.

My favorite of all the ghetto places I was forced to stay in was my aunt Fuzzy's house. Fuzzy was my mother's sister and the mother of my cousins Lisa and Punch. Lisa and Punch were about the same age as Rachel and me. We spent a lot of time at Aunt Fuzzy's house – months at a time. Fuzzy took us school shopping, taught us how to be young women, helped with homework, fed us, everything. Fuzzy was more of a mom to me than my actual mom during these years. Fuzzy had fried, curly, blonde hair and was 150lbs overweight. She never wore makeup and didn't dress up because she didn't care about appearance. Fuzzy ran the projects. Everyone knew who she was. And I'm not exaggerating when I say projects here. Fuzzy lived in government subsidized row housing in Connellsville, Pennsylvania. No one messed with Fuzzy because Fuzzy was a big bitch, and she'd kick your ass in a heartbeat.

There are so many reasons I loved staying there. The most important reason was that Fuzzy had food stamps. Lots of them! Which meant she always had food. Which meant all the pink lemonade in a gallon jug you could drink, imitation crab meat for days, processed American cheese. Bread, cookies, crackers, donut holes. Everything a fat eight-year-old girl could ever wish for. And Fuzzy let us eat whatever the hell

40

we wanted because she knew that for six months before we got to her, we were having to rob people on the streets to get a bite of a sandwich.

Another perk to staying at Fuzzy's house was that she let us do whatever we wanted. Not that I wasn't used to that, but it was like you didn't even have to try and hide shit from Fuzzy. We watched scary movies and listened to rock and roll. It was like a rule. You had to love Bad Company and Guns 'N' Roses or you weren't welcome. At one point, my cousin Lisa and I wrote letters to Axl and Slash telling them how much we loved them and that we would drop everything going on in our lives if they would just come marry us. We were eight, and we totally believed this was a possibility. We tried extra hard to make sure our grammar and punctuation was on point so they would think we were older and more mature. They never showed up or wrote back. Fuzzy took us to the mountains and drove fast on the roads where the cliffs dropped off beside us. We'd blast *Shooting Star* and *Ready for Love*, and we'd sing every word. We watched Point Break every day and played in the tiny ghetto front yard, standing on the transformers pretending to skydive like Bodhi and Johnny Utah. We longed to be bank robbers who wore presidential masks and surfed in our free time. We kept the TV on all night and fell asleep watching I Love Lucy.

We fought like cats and dogs, mostly because Rachel and Punch would fight, so Lisa and I had to stick up for our little sisters. Then inevitably Lisa and I would fist fight. I remember one time, Punch stabbed Rachel in the nipple with a fork. No shit. It was sticking in her boob. I yelled at Punch. Lisa yelled at me. We went tumbling down the plastic stairs bouncing each other's heads off of each step. She tried to drown me in the fish tank at the bottom of the stairs, so I threw her into the lit Christmas tree. And we eventually returned upstairs, exhausted, to find Rachel and Punch playing like nothing ever happened, so we decided to follow suit.

Lisa and Punch's father was named Ronnie. Fuzzy never married him. That was also probably a good call. My uncle Ronnie was tall and thin, and he had scars all over his face from an apparent radiator explosion when he was younger. My aunt Fuzzy and Uncle Ronnie took us to the flea market one day. Ronnie gave the four of us $2 apiece. What kind of trouble can four kids get into with a total of $8 at a flea market? Well, I'll tell you. We decided we had to get the biggest bang for our buck at this flea market, so we walked all around and looked at everything before making a purchase. Then we saw it, bright and shining with a white halo around it: A fucking chicken coop with baby chicks.

Me: "Sir, how much for these here baby chicks?"

Chicken guy: "$1.00 apiece."

Me: "Sir, how would you feel about selling these baby chicks for $0.50 a piece knowing that they'll be taken care of real good?"

Chicken guy: "Well, young lady, I guess I could go for that".

Me: "Thank you, Sir! We'll take $8 worth!"

The very kind chicken guy put all sixteen baby chicks in a box, and we went back to meet up with aunt Fuzzy and Uncle Ronnie. We showed Uncle Ronnie what we got with all our loot. We figured we did pretty well returning with sixteen whole live animals, but he was pissed! He said that we had to return the baby chicks immediately, but we cried and told him there were no refunds, so he let us keep them. He was such a pushover. I once heard a story that he may have killed a man. He didn't want to go to jail, so he hid in the mountains for several years. He ultimately did end up going to jail, though - for drugs. "What happened to the chicks?" you ask. We dropped them off at my mean grandma's house and made her take care of them. Revenge!

Some days were so fun, they made me forget I was in the projects. Other days, we would get bullied by the older girls or have an adult come to the door to ask us if we knew anyone who sold crack. Most days I forgot about my mom, but some days we'd miss her, Rachel especially. She'd beg me to call her. I think my mother purposely made us stay with poor people because she knew they wouldn't have long distance calling so we had to call collect. I'd dial 0, wait for the beep then say "Marlee". I'd wait for about two minutes, and the lady would come on saying "Your call has been rejected". Every time. We had no way of getting ahold of our mother. Even at eight years old, I knew she was rejecting our calls. And I'd lie to my baby sister and tell her that mom must not be home and that we'd try again later. I'd spend the rest of the day trying to distract her so that she wouldn't want to call again. And then one day – days, weeks, months later, my mom would show up, thin and beautiful with her blonde hair and her cool shades and her cool clothes and her cool car. And we'd be so happy.

There was a little black girl in the projects that my mom adored. Her name was Deborah. I don't know why my mother singled her out, but she did. For some reason, she felt obligated to take care of this little girl. My mom used to stop in at Fuzzy's and see us and say, "OK I'm going to take Deborah to the store, then I'll be back after that". She'd take her and buy her clothes and shoes and candy. And Deborah deserved it because she was a poor little girl who has probably grown up to not have much, but I remember always thinking that was very odd. I remember being jealous of that poor little girl. But I was always grateful that my mom had finally come to get us and that we could finally go home. I do hope that Deborah and all the other little girls who grew up in those projects have gotten everything they've wanted out of life, but I know the chances of that are slim. Those projects hold a special place in my heart because of my childhood there. Because that was the place where, at eight years old, I learned about real life. And also because six years later, I'd sneak down there from my friend's house and have my first kiss. He was ugly and an idiot, and it was terrible, so it was a fitting circumstance for my first kiss.

"Promise me you will not spend so much time treading water and trying to keep your head above the waves that you forget, truly forget, how much you have always loved to swim."

-Tyler Knott Gregson

Momma was a Rollin' Stone

I guess my mother had decided we'd lived in Pittsburgh long enough because one day, she came into our room and told Rachel and me that we were moving. We had three days to pack our things and tell our friends goodbye. My best friend was named Tiffany. She went to Catholic school with me. We'd been in the same class since kindergarten, and now we were in second grade. I would often escape to Tiffany's house to get a little taste of normalcy. Plus, her mom made us kick-ass Velveeta cheese dip with nachos or popcorn or any other thing you can dip in cheese, which is pretty much anything. I remember telling myself that I had to be as sweet as possible when I went to other people's houses because if I was extra nice, there was a chance they would feed me. Tiffany's parents fed me all the time.

Anyway, we're moving away to Connellsville, Pennsylvania – close to Fuzzy's house. We had no idea why. My mom said it was for "an adventure!" But the real reason was that she had apparently fallen in love with the big tall constable guy you read about a few chapters ago – the one who beat up my brother. We'll call him Baboon. And Baboon had a son. He was probably twenty. We'll call Baboon's son Orangutan.

I don't remember much about living with Baboon and Orangutan. I do remember our first day of school there. My mom thought it was adequate to drive us down to the school (ten blocks away) one time in her car to show us the route so that we could walk the following morning. Well, that morning was a disaster. I got about three blocks down the road and had made one turn and realized I didn't know where I was. And that a once-around drive was not adequate to send a seven- and an eight-year-old alone on foot to their brand-new school. We were lost for hours before finally finding our way back home. Baboon was watching TV when we got there. He asked why the fuck we weren't at school. I tried to explain. He didn't want to hear it. That was our first introduction to a belt across our asses. That was also the day I decided I hated Baboon, and it was also the day I decided I would eventually poison his morning coffee with *The Works* toilet bowl cleaner. I never actually did it, but I did also have that plan for two future stepfathers. I never got around to completing those tasks either.

One day, Baboon found out that my mom had also been sleeping with Orangutan, so Baboon shot Orangutan with his police-issued pistol. Thankfully (or not), the bullet was a blank round. But it made for an interesting show, nonetheless. We moved out the following morning, and I was grateful.

My mom had apparently been planning our escape for a while because she had already purchased her own house about eight blocks from Baboon's. It was old and disgusting, and she hired my brother Jason and his friends to fix it up for us. I had my first sip of beer while sitting in that shitty house eating take-out pizza and inhaling drywall dust with a bunch of construction workers. There was no running water, so everyone figured Rachel and me could drink beer with our pizza just like everyone else.

If not for pizza, I probably would have died of starvation as a child. Perhaps the best thing I learned to do as a child was learning to forge my mother's signature. Once I located my mom's stash of unopened checkbooks, I ordered food at least once a week. And what did I order? Breadsticks and ranch dressing. Because when you're ten years old sneaking around just trying to feed yourself and your little sister, nutrition just isn't a priority. And it hadn't been at any point in my life, so this was no different. I don't know if my mom ever found out about those missing checks. Or maybe she did, but she felt too guilty to question us about it because she knew it was for survival purposes. The forging of signatures would also play a huge role seven years later in my mandatory visit to the local magistrate for truancy and absenteeism from high school. I wrote myself school excuses probably once weekly because I hated school. The irony now is that my signature is exactly the same as my mother's. Don't feel bad for my mom. She would later forge my signature to get a line of credit for herself, using me as a cosigner. I knew nothing about it until debt collectors started calling me at work. Sometimes it's a shitty thing that the people who have raised you also get to know your social security number.

Shortly after Baboon was out of the picture, Marcina had fallen in love with her sixth husband. My Pappy Joe had always joked and said "where does she find these guys!? Outside the county jail?" Well this may have been true for husband number six because I have family photos of the four of us (him, my mom, Rachel, and me) with the Somerset County Prison family room as the backdrop. I always found it amusing that my mother had decided to date a constable and then immediately turn around and marry a convict. I don't know why this guy ended up in prison. He wasn't incarcerated when she met him. He had been in jail before and during their marriage, and he did end up there after she was done with him. One night in the now-fixed-up shitty house, number six had apparently spent a little too much time dabbling in the booze. There was some arguing which led to number six attempting to slap my mom which in turn led to my mom knocking him out cold with a frying pan. He was wearing whitey tighties and nothing else. He had come-to by the time the police got there, and he answered the door in those whitey tighties. They arrested him immediately. Rachel and I

47

sat on the steps and watched this whole thing occur. I have never seen number six again, and I'm grateful.

When I was half way through the sixth grade, we moved back to Pittsburgh. My mom still owned the house there, and she enrolled us back in our Catholic school. I met a new friend in my class that year. She had her nose pierced and listened to Marilyn Manson. She was eleven years old. She had red hair, pale skin, and black combat boots. She always talked to me about mosh pits and raves. I didn't know what the hell those were, but she was unlike any other person I'd ever known before, so I acted like I knew all about them. And I acted like I enjoyed listening to Marilyn Manson, even though I knew I was going to Hell for it. I always said a couple of extra Hail Marys after hanging out with her, just in case. We're still Facebook friends, which means we're not friends at all. She has since become a little less edgy, and I, in turn, have three whole Marilyn Manson songs on my iPod.

"Other people call me a rebel, but I just feel like I'm living my life and doing what I want to do. Sometimes people call that rebellion, especially when you're a woman."

-Joan Jett

Sugar, Spice, and Everything Naughty

The transition from elementary school to junior high is terrible. It is atrocious if you're coming from Catholic school. I knew five other people who would be leaving Catholic school and coming to junior high with me. The rest of those suckers had to go to mandatory Thursday morning mass until the end of 8th grade! Our junior high school was in the same building as the high school. This is a terrible idea. I remember trying to remain optimistic about going to junior high, but I also remember that I was just scared shitless. In homeroom on the first day of school, we were given our class schedules. My schedule went something like this:

Homeroom
Pre-Algebra
Study hall
Reading
Study hall
Lunch
Study hall
Science
Study hall

I knew something was wrong, but I figured I'd just ride this out. I had more study halls than I had classes, which would mean no homework. Ever. You might look at me in my line of work now and think I'm some kind of overachiever, but you'd be wrong. When it came to school, I was always a slacker. I did as little as I had to so that I could keep good enough grades to eventually get into college and get the hell out of my living situation.

Two of my study halls were in the cafeteria and two were in the auditorium. It's day three, study hall number three: I have nothing to do in my study hall. It was starting to get boring, so I decided to scope out the other people in my study hall and see what they were doing. Most of them were older. For some reason, my eyes fixated on a tall girl with an abnormally tiny head. She had blonde hair up to her shoulders and dark eye makeup. She was really unfortunate looking. I smiled at her. I figured we would go ahead and be friends. She gave me an "I'm going to kill you" look which caused me to immediately change my mind about ever being her friend. And at that point, I also changed my mind about having four study halls. So the next day, I confessed to the guidance counselor that I was given a schedule with four study halls. I should have also confessed about my post-traumatic stress from that bitch giving me a dirty look because obviously it still affects me, otherwise it wouldn't be in this book. Anyway, they yanked three of my study halls. They filled them in with a social studies, a world history, and a shop class. Everyone else was given a home economics class that year. I had shop class twice. I still blame my lack of cooking skills, cleaning skills, and my inability to know how to be a woman in general on this fucked up seventh grade schedule.

I was bullied a lot in junior high. I was going through an awkward phase. So was everyone else in my class, but I didn't realize that this happens to every junior high kid until way later. Some of the other awkward junior high kids decided to be assholes and pick on me. The biggest asshole was named Brian. That's not really his name, but we'll call him that for his safety. Brian was obviously a prick. And he was also terribly overweight. And not handsome at ALL! But for some reason, Brian felt it appropriate to call me names and always try to grab my vagina. He never actually got to it because thankfully, at some point, I learned to be very protective of my vagina. I have no idea how I decided to not be promiscuous because I know that based on my upbringing, I shouldn't have that trait. I remember hating Brian for his repetitive attempted vagina grabs. And I remember also wanting to poison him. But then one day, something amazing happened. We were in U.S. history or world history or one of those history classes that I obviously didn't pay attention to. Brian decided to leave my crotch alone for the day to try and go for Annie's. Annie was a tough chick. She seemed to have grown up a lot faster than the rest of us. I think she'd had a rough life. Plus, she wore a D cup by the time we got to eighth grade which made me wonder why Brian ever even thought about my vagina versus hers. Brian must have said something mean to Annie because Annie threatened to kill him right there in the middle of class. Brian said, "What did you say, bitch". And without hesitation, Annie stood up and slapped him as hard as she could in the face. And then she punched him over and over in the head until he fell out of his desk. He managed to stand up, and the fight moved outside the classroom into the hall. It went on for a surprisingly long time. None of the teachers wanted to break it up, partly because they knew Brian was a dick, and partly because they were all male teachers, and I think they were afraid of accidentally touching Annie's D cups. But they shouldn't have been afraid because something tells me those D cups had probably been touched by a teacher or two before. The fight eventually ended, and Brian laid on the floor sobbing. And it was one of the best fucking days of my life. Revenge!

By this time, Rachel was also now a student at the junior high, and she was rapidly becoming much more popular than me. Rachel had this friend, and they had a falling out. For whatever reason, Rachel and her friend had an argument that ultimately ended with each one making fun of the other because their father was a heroin addict, which was completely true in both cases. But I guess kids are sensitive about that sort of thing. So I, being the rational human being that I am, told Rachel's friend, "Well it's really not a big deal because it's actually true in both of your situations, and that's OK". Rachel's friend immediately told his older sister that I called her father a heroin addict. Our home phone rang an hour later, and the girl on the other end asked for me. My mom tells me my friend is on the phone.

Marlee (excited): "Hello!??" (Shut up. That may have actually been my first ever phone call.)

Julia: "Did you call my fucking dad a heroin addict!?"

Marlee (Oh my GOD!): "What? Who is this?" (Knowing damn well who it was.)

Julia: "This is Julia. And I know what you said to my little brother. So you BETTER be ready to fuckin' fight tomorrow in school!" Click.

So, I peed in my pants a little, and I ran to find Rachel. By this time, she was a black belt in Tae Kwon Do. I explained what had just happened, and Rachel laughed at me. She wasn't afraid to fight. She was always beating people up. I'd seen her knock three people unconscious with one punch by this point. I, on the other hand, was still trying to find myself and spent most afternoons reading The Babysitter's Club and removing glitter glue from the pads of my fingers. So Rachel finally decided to show me how to fight. She said the first thing I had to accomplish was to develop my stance. She said I had to stand solid, so she spent twenty minutes making me stand with my feet shoulder width apart, knees slightly bent, one foot in front of the other so she could push me around and make sure I didn't fall over. I should have already known all of this because I, too, was a Tae Kwon Do master, although I only ever made it to yellow belt, which is one step past a white belt, which is the beginner belt, which is like a total of three months in karate. OK so maybe not a "master".

We never actually made it to practicing the real fighting part. I was pretty exhausted after learning my stance, and I figured that was good enough, so we decided to call it a night. Morning came, and it was time for me to face my fear. Looking back, I probably could have written myself a school excuse for the day and signed my mom's name on it, but I wasn't quite as bright back then. First period – no Julia. Second – in the clear. Third – good. Lunch – fine. Right after lunch, I'm walking by the front office, and she says, "Oh! There you are!"

Marlee: (Oh man. I want to run. I want to pee. I want to cry too, but I can't do that.) "Yeah, BITCH! Here I am! Now what!!?" (Oh my God I can't believe that just came out of my mouth!)

Julia: "Oh look at you. Standing up for yourself."

Marlee: (Don't say a word. Don't ruin it. Don't cry.)

Julia: "Nice." (Walks away)

Marlee: (What the fuck!? Did that just happen!?)

From that moment on, every time Julia saw me in the halls, she'd smile or say "what's up" or go out of her way to acknowledge me. It was in that moment that I became a badass. And I don't even know where it came from. Maybe it was the Pittsburgh in me. Maybe it was because I had decided I was done taking shit from bullies. I made the cheerleading squad that year, too…for wrestling. So I made the reject cheerleading squad. You gotta start somewhere.

Later that year, I was quoted in the local newspaper for complaining about how all the older girls would smoke cigarettes in the school bathrooms, and they'd talk mean to us if we tried to go in and pee. I said it was the most horrible thing ever, and I would never ever smoke. Fast forward 2 years, and I was smoking in every single bathroom in that school, but I was never mean to anyone.

I spent that summer with my friend Pia. Pia lived in Connellsville. She was the only real friend I ever made in Connellsville. I loved Pia, and I loved her parents. And they loved me too, like I was their own daughter. Pia's dad was black and her mom was white. I like to contribute the little bit of *flavor* in my life to hanging out at Pia's house. The first time I met P's parents, I went to their house to visit. I was wearing a skirt and pantyhose, and I have no idea why. I don't dress like that. And I shouldn't have dressed like that back then, either, because Pia's cat took one look at me and immediately attacked my pantyhose like they were a scratching post. I screamed and ran, and there was blood all over their floor.

Pia's grandmother also lived with them. We called her Mimi. Mimi was 114 years old. That's an exaggeration, but she was definitely pushing ninety. Mimi smoked a pack of Virginia Slims per day. She drank a cup of hot tea every night before bed and every morning for breakfast. I never saw her eat anything. She knitted all day long, but she wasn't one of those sweet little knitting ladies. She was mean as fuck. So, the secret to longevity is to knit, smoke rather than eat, drink hot tea, and be a bitch. I could never give up the eating part, so I guess I'll die young.

That summer with Pia was another very important moment in my journey to becoming a woman. Pia and I decided we should become smokers, so we rolled up a bunch of Post-It notes and lit the ends on fire and puffed on them - which is why not only will I die young, I will die young from lung cancer. Post-It notes don't stay lit, so we decided to steal cigarettes here and there from Mimi. We took cigarettes to the playground by her house and made sure we smoked them around anyone who would watch us. A couple puffs here and there. We weren't good at it. I had also started my period that summer, had my first kiss, and stole my first car. Relax. It was Pia's idea, and it was her dad's work van. It was not a "cool ride". It had *Montgomery Ward* written all across the side of it. We were 14, and even though she was six months younger than me, Pia knew how to drive - or at least that's what she told me that night. She actually drove really well, and we even passed a police car. They didn't suspect a thing. We finally came home and were super quiet getting out of the van. We walked in the front door, and Pia's mom was waiting for us in the living room. It was 4 a.m. She was more upset than I'd ever seen her, which meant that she slightly raised her voice while talking to us. Pia and I got grounded for the first time ever (at Pia's house. I had been grounded many times at home before that). We were grounded from 4:15 a.m. to 2 p.m., which is when we finally woke up. Pia's mom was taking a nap, so we got in her bed and snuggled with her and begged her to take away our sentence. And we also let her know that it would be cool if we could have $5 apiece to walk to the corner store to get a hoagie. We were cleared of our charges and scored the $5 apiece. Miss Dee was the ultimate pushover.

It was a little difficult to say goodbye to Pia that summer. You'd think with all the times I'd been dropped off at someone's house against my will, I'd never want to go anywhere, but by this point, I was a total nomad. I hated my house, but it was time to go back to Pittsburgh. I was home for five hours, and I started to feel really agitated. Initially I couldn't figure out why, but then it hit me. I need a cigarette! Luckily, my mom smoked. I took a cigarette out of her pack, and went down into the basement to take a couple puffs. I heard the door open. I saw my life flash before my eyes. I was definitely going to be grounded for more than ten hours if my mom caught me. I put out my cigarette and pretended to do laundry, which consisted mostly of Corey's underwear.

Rachel: "What are you doing down here?"

Me: "Laundry, duh!" (I thought this was a plausible explanation because we'd been forced to do laundry since we

55

were six. We started doing dishes at age three. The only reason my mother had children was to have a small army of little people to do chores.)

Rachel: "I smell smoke."

Me: (Fuck.) "I don't know. Must be from mom."

Rachel: "Mom's not home. Oh! There it is!"

Rachel picked up my half-smoked cigarette and the lighter from the floor, lit the cigarette, and started puffing it like a pro.

Me: "Oh my God! What are you doing!? I'm telling mom."

Rachel: "Go ahead. You're guilty too. I've been smoking for years. It's cool."

And that is when I realized that my baby sister was more of a G than I'll ever be.

"The first cut is the deepest."

-Sheryl Crow

"That is a terrible fucking song, but it's so catchy."

-Me

Sex, Drugs, and More Stepdads

High School Algebra: A wonderful blend of awkward, intelligent, prepubescent girls and ridiculously stupid, horny, older boys who collectively want to pass this mandatory math class. At least that's what my experience was like. Travis sat behind me in algebra. He was not smart, but he was a star football player, and he was handsome, and he was older. Travis fancied my friend Courtney, but that didn't stop him from flirting with me so that I'd let him cheat off my tests, and I did. Travis told me I should spend all my Christmas money on a big huge sack of weed for the weekend, so I did. Then he told me I should do the same with my birthday money a few weekends later, so I did. Travis thought it would be a good idea for me to date his best friend, so I did. His best friend was short and had bad acne and a big head. I fell in love almost immediately.

He was shy, which was charming. And he loved marijuana, which was fucking terrible. This guy needs a name, so for his protection, we'll call him Ross. He was seventeen, and I was fourteen. We didn't even kiss for like two months. I thought that was nice of him, but I was ready to get it on, so much so that I told my mom.

Me: "I want to lose my virginity to Ross". (You may think this is weird, but my mother encouraged me to let her know as soon as I felt like I was ready to lose my virginity so we could do like every good Catholic girl does and get on birth control.)

Mom: "Oh honey that's so exciting! You're becoming a woman! I'll go call Dr. Smith and we'll get you an appointment.

I don't recommend this type of talk with your daughter. I mean, I recommend speaking openly about sex, but don't tell her you're excited she's becoming a woman because she wants to give up her V card. Tell her she's becoming a woman when she exercises her right to the 19th amendment or something. That way she can be proud of it instead of equating womanhood with whoring around.

Ross convinced me that it was totally cool for me to sleep at his house one night, so I brought my cute little PJs and went along. At 2 a.m., his stepfather came into his room and saw an extra foot poking out of the blanket - a girl foot. MY foot. That was the first time I'd met Ross's stepfather and mother so naturally, they hated me. It turns out, I wasn't allowed to sleep over after all. Ross's stepfather had to drive me all the way home at three in the morning. That was a long, awkward ride. Ross's mom thought for sure I'd be grounded for this little episode until I showed up the next day at his baseball game.

Ross's mom: "Ross is grounded for three months! Why are you out of your house?!"

Me: "Oh. I'm not grounded."

Ross's mom: "Do you even have a mother?"

I honestly didn't know how to answer that question. That's not the only time I've been asked that question, and I never knew how to answer it because I was never really sure of the answer. My many tardy appearances to high school prompted the attendance officer to often ask similar questions. "Do you not have someone sending you to school? Do you really think you're going to graduate!? Do you not have a hat and mittens?" "Naw, bitch. I don't wear *mittens!*" Just kidding. I never said that. She did take me to court once. The magistrate threw out the case because my grades were so good. Rachel was not so lucky. I hated that attendance officer. I vowed to one day have a job that was much more important than hers. Oh if she could see me now. I'm going to send her an autographed copy of this book. She may actually be dead by now. She was old. Maybe that's why she said *"mittens"*.

I knew within about three months that Ross and I were just not going to make it. We dated for three more years. I was always getting upset about his weed addiction, so I'd break up with him. Then I'd get lonely, so I'd go back after him, and naturally, he couldn't resist. This happened about 53 times because we were sixteen and eighteen, and we were so in love. One day, I was on my way to chase him with a bouquet of roses in my hand. I had walked about a mile in wedge heels to tell him I was sorry for breaking up with him. I knocked on the door to his apartment. No answer. I knew he was home because his friend told me he had just dropped him off. I climbed up the fire escape to the back door. I opened the back door, and I saw Ross sitting in his living room with two girls. They were all on opposite sides of the room, and none of them were anywhere near each other. The lights were nearly all out, and they were just sitting there in a daze. I walked in and walked back out immediately. I later found out that they had just all dropped acid about thirty minutes prior to my arrival. That was my last attempt at chasing after Ross.

Pretty close to this time, I got some kind of weird viral upper respiratory infection. It made me super sick. I remember having trouble walking up the stairs at one point because my legs were so weak. Two days after that, Rachel found me lying in bottom of the shower unconscious. My mom took me to see a neurologist. He ordered an EEG that came back normal and told my mom I was fine. A week later, during a snow storm, my mom carried me into his office. My legs wouldn't work, and I couldn't walk. She dumped me on the exam table and said, "Here! Tell me she's OK now!" He admitted me to the hospital immediately. I don't remember much about that experience. I had Guillain Barre Syndrome. It's a rare neurological disease that's thought to be from a viral illness. It can cause paralysis that can ultimately work its way up to the diaphragm and cause respiratory failure and death. When I had it, the paralysis only went to my waist. I remember it was a bizarre phenomenon to tell my toes to wiggle, but they wouldn't. I remember there was a handsome young resident doctor who asked me if he could do my lumbar puncture. I told him, "Yeah. You can do it. I want to be a doctor, too, and I'll have to find someone to let me do my first spinal tap on them". I don't remember my seventeenth birthday. Rachel tells me she had her friends come over and throw me a party with a cake and candles. I still have the little birthday cards they gave me, but I don't remember anything from that day. I had to leave school for the rest of my junior year. Three of my teachers volunteered their time to come and teach me at home. I still somehow ended up doing very well in my classes. I don't remember a thing. Some people who get this disease have lifelong lasting effects. I'm one of the lucky ones.

At some point in high school, my mom's friend "Blind Chris" moved in. It's OK that I call him that because that's what he called himself. He was about 5'7" and stocky. He had a receding hairline but long hair. He had a sweet-ass German Shepard. He got on the bus every day and went to college. He played the piano like Stevie Wonder. Literally, just like him. He made the best dippy eggs. I was amazed at what he could do even though he was blind. My mom tried to act like he was not our new "uncle", but that just wasn't true. He always had weed, which was good for Rachel because she always stole it from him and said, "You must have misplaced it". We played hide and seek with him, and he was surprisingly good at it. He said he could hear us breathe, which was bullshit because we held our breaths most of the time. I remember thinking it should be a piece of cake playing hide and seek with a blind guy, but it was not! He kicked our asses! Occasionally we snuck into his room and videotaped him while he was sleeping just to see if he could hear us, and we caught his reaction on tape when he woke up. He woke up every time. It was amazing. I don't know why we found that so entertaining because all it did was piss him off. We have footage of him rolling over yelling, "Girls! Get the fuck out of here! Why do you do this!?" I'm grateful for him coming into my life. He was one of the most normal men in my life. He was supportive and encouraged us to chase our dreams. So naturally, my mother kicked him out.

After Blind Chris, my mother started dating a weird guy whom she said favored Fabio. I say he favored Charles Manson much better. He had long brown hair, buck teeth, and fake gold earrings. He lived in a former train station that was about 500 square feet in total. I hated him from the moment I met him. He made it obvious that he had no interest in my mother's children. He was dumb. We used to call him Forrest Gump, but I hated doing that because I loved that movie. Everyone made fun of him. My mother was a smart lady. No one knew why she gave this guy the time of day. He had a beat-up car, no money, four dogs, and some fish. His earrings were tarnished, and that always bothered me more than anything else. My mother decided that we would move out of our 4 bedroom home and into his 500 square foot train station. 250 feet of that was dedicated to his dogs and fish. A large tarp covered the floors they pissed on. The house was 10 feet from an active railroad. I was NOT moving into that piece of shit with that piece of shit. "You'll be Homecoming queen at Avella High", they said. "I don't give two shits. I will be emancipated before I move into that hellhole." My mom thought I was lying, but I wasn't. By that time, the internet was a real thing, and I had looked up teen emancipation and how to get it done. We were scheduled to leave the next morning. I woke up, expecting to pack and move to Tarah's house, but we heard nothing more about moving in with Forrest Fabio. It was never spoken of again. Rumor has it that my mother spent that night with Heather, Jason's ex-girlfriend. Heather supposedly talked her out of it. However it happened, I'm grateful.

"Is it a crime, to fight, for what is mine?"

-Tupac Shakur

Daydream Believer or Homecoming Queen

It was the night before my first day of my senior year, and I was getting my clothes together so I could look fly for my first day of school. Corey was partying with his friends outside, and he wasn't supposed to be. He didn't even live there. My house was more hectic than usual during this time because my mom had married husband number seven, and they were out of town together all the time. They even decided to get married out of town, in another state - not because it was exotic, but because I think the state of Pennsylvania finally said, "No, bitch. No more marriage licenses." It was getting late, and Corey and his friends were being obnoxiously loud. I couldn't fall asleep. It was going to be my first day back to school in half a year, and I wanted to make an effort to be rested. I asked for them to be quiet, and Corey got pissed. He was trying to impress some girls. He ran down to me and punched me in the jaw, knocking my earring out. I cried, not because of the pain, but more because of the emotion behind it. I think he probably ultimately felt bad. My jaw still feels different on the right side than it does on the left. I didn't make it to school the next day. I did call the police that night, though, and they surprised Corey and company when they were sitting in the hot tub. It turns out Corey's friend had a warrant out for his arrest. Oops. Revenge!

By this time, I had finally made the football cheerleading squad. I was pretty good, too, because they made me a captain. Tarah was the other captain. I remember being so excited to go to our football games. But then the games would end, and I'd walk home all by myself. No one from my family ever came to see me cheer. I was really bummed about that. I had also scored some solos in chorus, but no one came to my concerts to see me sing either. My mom had given up on checking up on my grades and status in school. I guess she trusted me to just have it figured out or something. I stopped playing the saxophone, partly because the band instructor was a douche and partly because I had gotten my tongue pierced, and it's difficult to play a woodwind instrument with a hunk of metal in your mouth. Priorities.

I studied German for four years in high school and ended up going to Germany during my junior year. I managed to get into some mild trouble over there because my friend Tiffany and I found some Italian boys and snuck back to their room with them. They didn't speak a lick of English and of course, we didn't speak Italian. We just kind of sat around batting eyelashes and laughing. My German teacher found us and came in and totally killed the vibe. I didn't know anything about the trafficking of actual human beings at that time, or else I may have been more cautious. I had not yet seen the major motion picture *Taken*, so I just wasn't educated about it. I was the only one who was old enough to drink alcohol in Germany. But of course I didn't drink, so I just bought it for everyone else for a small fee. I had decided I would not be a drinker at age 14 when I decided to turn up a bottle of vodka in an experiment to see what being drunk felt like. I felt completely normal, walked halfway up the stairs in my house, and couldn't make it up the second half. When I finally did come-to a little, I made myself vomit and decided I'd be a nondrinker. That was the only time in my life I'd ever been drunk, and it will probably remain that way indefinitely.

Right before I left for Germany, I started dating this star football player. He was a year younger than me. We'll call him Chris. Chris was pretty similar to me. He was popular, smart, and he had tattoos. He was about 5'10" and wished he was taller. When he figured out that was impossible, he just decided he'd spend every day in the gym growing muscles instead. Everybody pretty much agreed we belonged together. I wasn't sure about him before I left for Germany, but I was sure I missed him while I was there, so we got pretty close when I got back. His mother hated me too.

The people in my high school ultimately decided that I should be the homecoming queen. That was a really cool moment. I was surprised. Corey was even more surprised. They announced my name, and Corey went crazy cheering for me. He was the one who walked me down the field when they announced the homecoming court. I don't think he could have ever believed I had become "cool". He took me out to dinner that night. Of course, it was at the place in which he worked so we could get a free meal, but that was OK. He paraded me around and introduced me to everyone and made me show off my crown. There were very few times when Corey showed me he was proud of me. That was one of them. I also remember when I was about fifteen, I was crying because Ross had broken my heart again. Corey wiped my tears and asked me, "Why are you crying over that asshole. You are the best thing he will ever have in his life. I hope he messes it up. You're too good for him. You are a diamond in the rough". I used to get terrible headaches when I had Guillain Barre Syndrome. Corey would massage my head for hours. We watched March Madness together the year that I was sick. We played video games all night long and would sleep all day.

When the yearbook came out, they had a list of people who were nominated "Senior Mosts". Apparently I had the nicest hair, nicest eyes, and was the friendliest. They didn't have a category for most stepdads, or else I would have won that one too.

There is a moment within my senior year that I'm not very proud of. We had a chorus concert rehearsal in the auditorium one day during school. A younger girl came up to me and told me she had just seen someone steal my purse. She said she followed her because she knew it was my purse and that the girl had taken it into the bathroom. I was furious. I ran out the door, down the halls, up the stairs, and into the bathroom. I heard the girl zipping and unzipping things. I went into the bathroom slowly, but I banged on her stall door.

Me: "Open up! You have my purse! You better open this door right now, or I'll come under the motherfucker! Give. Me. My. Shit!" (You see, I didn't have anything. I didn't own anything. And if she had really needed something, I would have been the first person to give it to her.)

Thief: "What? What are you talking about?!" (Now frantically zipping)

Me: "Bitch if you don't open this door, I'm going to KILL you! I'm coming under the door!"

Thief: "Oh my God. I'm scared!

She opened the door then ran over and cowered down in the corner behind the toilet. I continued to scream other obscenities, and Mrs. Mohr, my sweet little math teacher, came into the bathroom and said, "Marlee, I've never heard you talk like this. What is going on?"

Me: "She stole my shit, Mrs. Mohr. And I don't have shit, and I don't own shit."

Thief: "I'm so sorry."

I couldn't go after this girl now that Mrs. Mohr was in the room with us. Mrs. Mohr was 105 years old and always had lipstick on her teeth. And she was also one of the teachers who came to my home to teach me when I got sick.
   Do you know what the contents of my purse were? Some chap stick, 2 Marlboro menthol lights, a stick of black

eyeliner, some glitter, and a tube of coconut lime verbena lotion. Those were the contents of my purse, and they were essentially the contents of my life. I paid for them myself with money I probably got from carrying some old lady's groceries into her house for her. I was a hustler. Everything I had, I got for myself - except for my pistol. Thankfully that wasn't in there. I recovered almost everything from the thief, except the lotion. She had thrown that in the trash in an effort to get rid of the evidence, and I was so angry, I didn't even think to look for it.

The following morning at school surprised me. It surprised me because I had actually made it to school before the morning bell rang, but it also surprised me because the thief was able to roam free through the halls just one day after robbing the homecoming queen. I went to the principal (whom I knew very well) immediately.

Me: "Mr. Kyle, if you don't suspend that girl, I am going to beat her ass today. I tried to go about it the right way! I didn't beat her up yesterday. If you don't punish her, I will!"

Mr. Kyle: "Marlee, we spoke with her about suspension, but she was afraid that her parents would beat her if she got suspended."

Me: "Well she needs her ass beat, Mr. Kyle! Send her home. She needs beat!"

I ultimately felt sorry for that girl, not because she would get beat at home. She probably needed an ass-whoopin' for that thievery. I felt bad because I later found out that she was only in ninth grade, and she was brand new to our school. If I had known she was in ninth grade, I would have given her a swirly instead of making her feel like I was going to kill her. It's also sad to wonder what kind of person steals someone else's half-used bottle of lotion. I never saw that girl again after speaking with Mr. Kyle that day.

At this point, I had taken my SATs and applied to the colleges that I thought I wanted to attend. I was getting so close to reaching my dream of getting the hell out of my house. Acceptance letters started rolling in, and I was accepted to all the colleges I wanted to go to, including six extras that my mom decided to apply to for me. Apparently she just felt like submitting my information to places I'd never heard of to see if I could get in. She never told me she was doing it. I just found out when the letters came in. I have no idea why she did that. Maybe she was trying to get interested in my life because I was leaving soon.

When I turned eighteen, my mom did get me a job as a bartender at one of the bars on the North Side of Pittsburgh. Her best friend was the owner, and I hated drinking, so she thought I'd be a perfect fit. It was a fun job, and I made a lot of friends. Marci, the owner, was a short, tough Mexican chick. She always wore tight jeans, a vest, and a revolver on her hip. My mom and Marci decided that I needed a pistol too, so they took me gun shopping. I remember my mom telling me how great she was because she was going to be buying me a gun and how guns were expensive and how I should be grateful. I left that bar on the North Side at 3 a.m. with at least $150 cash every night. I was grateful for my pistol.

I graduated high school, despite almost failing every last-semester class because I stopped going to school as soon as I got my last acceptance letter for undergrad. I didn't wait for Marcina to get all of her acceptance letters. I skipped out of school a lot during my senior year. I knew all the teachers, and they let me do what I had to do, which was nothing. I skipped school so I could go home and sleep. I remember our graduation ceremony. My mom came to that, disposable camera in hand. I have all kinds of awesome blurred pictures of Tarah and me holding hands while singing "The Farewell Song" on stage. I graduated with honors.

"The most common lie is that which one lies to himself; lying to others is relatively an exception."

-Friedrich Nietzsche

Who's Your Daddy?

It was time for me to get my shit together because I was moving away to college. Westminster College was an hour and ten minutes away from my mom's house. I could still come home to do laundry. I would like to say I chose Westminster because it was my favorite college, but that would be a lie. I chose Westminster because it was the cheapest and because they gave me the most scholarship money. I also chose Westminster because Marcina somehow convinced me that she was paying for my undergraduate education, so I had better pick the cheapest one. I ended up graduating with $20,000 in student loan debt from Westminster. I didn't know I owed that until six months after graduation when Marcina was finally forced to fess up to her crime of lying to me about paying for my education because I started receiving the bill in the mail. Considering yearly tuition was $33,000 per year back then, I guess I did pretty well, but it still chaps my ass every time I send that monthly payment.

What does one need to go to college? Well, there are your dorm room necessities, such as your papasan chair, desk lamp, beanbag chair, large mirror, food, forks and such, etc. Marcina managed to get me all psyched up for a future trip to Bed Bath and Beyond. I found an advertisement, so I started circling the things I would need, complete with the hot pink lava lamp that I never got from selling candy bars in grade school. We went to store, and my mom gave me the budget when we got there, so I left with a total of one papasan chair and a towel.

69

What else does one need? Oh yeah! A driver's license. I had held out on getting a driver's license because everybody thought I was having seizures when I got super sick in high school. By the time they decided I was seizure-free, I was enjoyed being chauffeured around, so it was no longer a priority to get a license. But now it was time because I was going to college in two weeks. I put on my shortest shorts, and I went to the DMV for my appointment. I did awesome except that I pulled out in front of someone because I had been waiting at the stop sign for at least a minute. The instructor told me I shouldn't have done that to which I replied, "Well this is a real-life scenario, isn't it? By the way, do you like my shorts?" Just kidding. I didn't ask him if he liked my shorts. I already knew the answer to that! But come on! Give me a break! No one is going to sit at a stop sign for ten minutes waiting for traffic to clear! You pull out in front of the least-intimidating driver you see. Everybody knows that. I passed, probably because I reminded him ten times that I was leaving for college in two weeks, and failure was not an option. Or maybe because he may have been able to see my vagina. Either way, I was one step closer to freedom.

Now that I had a license, I needed a car. My mother insisted that we buy a car from the local Ford dealership. I want to tell you that my first car was a Mustang, but it was a Ford Contour. And it had been crashed before. And it was also in a flood, which was all information that my mother knew about that she never told me. I didn't find out until I was finally able to get rid of it. My mom convinced me that it was the coolest car ever. She put $500 down on it and told me she'd pay off the rest in $123 monthly payments. How do I know that exact dollar amount? Because Marcina only made a payment for two months before she decided she could no longer afford it. It's cool though because by that time, I was trying to hold down a part time job at a bar in Pittsburgh three nights a week and go to college, 80 miles away, full time.

Now I have a car and a license. My mom insisted on driving me to college on move-in day so that we could take her truck and load it up with all my stuff. We had lots of extra room after loading up the papasan chair, some clothes, and my towel. My mom had started to tell me that she was proud of me for going to college and that she would miss me. I reminded her that I had to return home with her that night and that I would also be home on Friday to do my laundry, so it really wasn't a big deal. We got about thirty miles up the highway, and my mom started sobbing out of nowhere.

Me: "Jesus Christ, Mom. What the hell is going on?"

Marcina: "Oh, Marlee, I have something to tell you, and I don't want you to hate me for it. It's embarrassing, and I just know you're going to hate me."

Me: "Don't be dramatic, mom. What's up?" (Please don't think I lack empathy. These sobbing outbursts had occurred quite frequently in my life. My mother was the only woman I have ever known to have had a self-proclaimed fifteen year-long menopause.)

Marcina: "Marlee...Denny is not your dad."

Me: (What in the FUCK are you talking about!??!?) "Oh wow. Really?"

Marcina: "PLEASE DON'T HATE ME!"

Me: (You selfish bitch.) "Mom, calm down. So who is my dad then?"

Marcina: "His name is Pete Popowicz, and he's lived in Brookline your entire life. He was a heroin addict when you were conceived, and he was really hooked on it. He wouldn't have been good for you, and I met Denny very shortly after I found out I was pregnant with you, and Denny promised he would take care of you and love you like you were his own."

71

Me: (I want to rip your fucking head off!) "Hm. OK. Well it's ok. I thought my dad was dead anyway, so it's not like it makes a difference."

I don't remember how the rest of that conversation went. I just remember feeling like my mother was fragile at that moment and that I had to protect her, from myself. I had had that feeling many times in the past and would have it many more times in the future. We dropped off my few things in my new dorm room, and I met my new roommates. I was supposed to have had a roommate named Shaniqua, and I remember thinking we would totally end up being besties, but Shaniqua never showed up, so I was left with Alexis and Alexis. One had blonde hair and one had brown hair.

My mom and I didn't say much on the ride home. I guess we just sat and thought a lot. I had to continuously tell myself not to lash out, not to lose my cool. It felt like we were in that car for five hours. We finally made it home. I went upstairs to the bathroom. I drew myself a bath, stepped in, and collapsed. I was sobbing. I can't even explain what I felt in that moment. I felt like I had been living an eighteen-year lie, but it was bigger than that. I felt like I didn't belong anywhere. I felt like I was just starting to learn my worth and just starting to feel important. I felt like it was all ripped away at once. Suddenly, I didn't have any idea who I was or where I came from. I thought about how I would tell my sister that we were not of the same blood. We thought we were the only ones of all our siblings who had matching parents, and that was important to us. I thought about how I had interacted for all this time with this whole family of wonderful people who weren't even my relatives and how they would react when they found out. I thought about how I wanted to belong to them because they were at least somewhat normal. I thought about how my mother marched into a tattoo shop with me when I was turning sixteen to sign a paper that said I could get a tattoo in memory of my late father who was not even my father at all. I thought about how she knew he wasn't my dad, and she let me get that tattoo. And I thought about how she was selfish and that this was the story of my life. I knew it wasn't fair that I felt responsible for protecting her emotions even though she was the mother. And then I thought that I had better stop feeling sorry for myself because there were many people who had it much worse than me. I started to feel grateful to be able to have that bathtub full of warm, running water. I remembered that I was now a college student, and I was well on my way to a life I would make for myself.

"The woman who does not require validation from anyone is the most feared individual on the planet."

-Mohadesa Najumi

College Education I'm Still Paying For

During my second week of college, I was driving back to school for a class in the morning after working at the bar the night prior, and it was raining heavily. Consequently, I was jamming out to Millie Vanilli's "Blame it on the Rain". I don't know what happened exactly, but my car started spinning out of control. I landed on an embankment off the highway after crashing into the guardrail twice. The airbags deployed, and I couldn't see anything. I thought maybe I had died, but then I heard my horn constantly beeping. I opened the car door and fell out of the car onto the wet grass in the fetal position and yelled, "Mom!!!" Then I immediately realized I looked like an idiot and stood up and brushed myself off. She did come to rescue me, but I was completely fine. And unfortunately, the piece of shit car was not totaled.

Things were going well with Alexis Blonde and Alexis Brown. We were living the college life: eating Easy Mac out of melted, Styrofoam bowls, packing on the pounds, hanging out at the frat houses, encouraging each other to make all the bad decisions we'd ever tried in our own individual lives. But no matter how much time I spent on my studies, I was struggling in school. My GPA after my first semester was 2.7. I had never had a GPA below 3.8. I was trying to balance school with fun and work, and it was hard! I majored in Biology because that's the only thing I liked. I would later go on to take so many history classes that I almost had a history minor. I quit going out with the Alexises so that I could study harder.

That landed me a GPA of 2.8 the second semester. I went to school for sometimes eight hours per day, Monday through Friday, and I worked at the bar back in Pittsburgh every Tuesday, Friday, and Saturday night. Tuesday was pool night, so it was good money, but it meant that I either showed up half asleep or not at all for my 0800 chemistry class on Wednesdays. I also started missing my 0900 psychology class. The chemistry professor liked me, so he didn't dock me for missing class. My psychology professor gave me a C-, even though I made A's on all of her tests. I decided to get psychological with her ass. I told her that I deserved the A because that's what my coursework reflected. I also told her that I was working at a bar back in Pittsburgh three days a week so that I could afford my car payment, car insurance, food, and so that I could put myself through school. I managed to conjure up a few tears, so she gave me an A-.

That is when I learned that life is all about the gift of gab. Just because someone is a college professor does not mean she is not human. I used a similar technique when I decided to take two organic chemistry classes as summer courses the following year. I knew I would suck at organic chemistry, so I had to find a way around actually doing well in the class. It turned out the professor was an old man who spoke German, so I shot the shit with him in German every day. I failed every test but ended up with a C+ in both classes. I showed up to that class every day, and even though I fucked everything up in nearly every lab session, I was very enthusiastic about learning. I did get the "let's make moonshine" lab right!

These mediocre grades gave me the boost I needed to start believing in myself and doing better in my classes. I never had lower than a 3.5 GPA for the rest of my college career. Things were getting easier regarding school, but things got shaky between the Alexises. One day, Alexis Blonde drove to Alexis Brown's house and beat her up while she was throwing a house party. Alexis Brown's entire family was there, but Alexis Blonde still managed to beat her up. Alexis Brown's family was Italian! I do not understand how that happened. If you know Italian families, you know this should not be possible, but somehow it was. Shortly thereafter, I decided to move into an apartment with Alexis Blonde.

Her father owned the apartment building we lived in. It was really nice, but it wasn't quite finished. School was starting soon, so we had to move in. We would not be waiting for a shower or toilet installation. We took showers at Alexis' mom's house about ten minutes away. We used a five gallon bucket as a toilet for 4 months. One time, I even took a dump outside in the yard. I have since learned how to set my own damn toilet.

So many interesting things happened in that apartment, the most bizarre of which happened on the night I trusted Alexis to babysit my chinchilla Pollo. Pollo was a white chinchilla who was a complete fucking bastard. Prior to purchasing Pollo, we bought Quesadilla, our sweet little baby girl chinchilla. We had thought Pollo was a girl chinchilla also until we woke up one morning, and we had two extra chinchillas in the cage. I promptly learned that chinchillas are a hot commodity at universities and that people would pay $120 apiece for them. Breeding Pollo and Quesadilla became a routine occurrence. Relax. I only did it like twice, or maybe three times. One day, Alexis was babysitting Pollo. You may be asking how much trouble one can get into while babysitting a caged animal. Well, let me tell you. Alexis decided that Pollo was feeling cooped up, so she let him out of his cage. This is fine because we did it all the time. However, on this particular evening, Alexis had forgotten that the floor-level vent cover in the bathroom had been removed, leaving a perfect chinchilla-sized hole for lots of exciting maze-running all through the vent system of the apartment building. Alexis thought nothing more of Pollo's activity and went to bed. When I came home, our apartment smelled horribly like burnt hair. I asked Alexis if she'd just used the blow dryer. She hadn't. Then it clicked. I knew what it was. Pollo must have dropped down into the furnace, and he was dead and still burning. I made Chris look in the furnace, but he couldn't see anything. I tried to go to sleep, but I was too worried. I started hearing scratching in the floor. I just knew it was Pollo. Chris checked the furnace again, and this time he saw Pollo. We took the entire furnace apart, and we found Pollo sitting there under the heating coils shaking. He looked like a roasted marshmallow, but he was breathing. We rushed him to the emergency veterinarian. They charged me $290 to tell me he was fine, and they gave me a cup of burn cream to put on his little ears, feet, and penis. I'm pretty sure I'm still paying interest on my credit card for that emergency vet visit. Pollo was a dick before that. He was noticeably sweeter after.

Alexis and I took a ton of road trips in my shitty Ford Contour. One such trip was a trip to New Orleans pretty shortly after hurricane Katrina. After the hurricane hit, my mom, Rachel, Corey, and Jason moved there to be general contractors because apparently things were so shitty down there, all you had to do was flash your nursing license, and they'd let you pour a concrete slab and build a house. I remember one time, while I was visiting in New Orleans, Corey prank called my mother pretending to be an Asian man who needed a new roof. My mom also had a roofing company down there.

Corey: "Harro".

Mom: "Hello there!"

Corey: "Uh yeah uhhh…hi. I need wubba woof."

Mom: "I'm sorry. I can barely hear you. I'm driving. Here…let me pull over." (Pulls off highway, shuffles papers)

Corey: "Yes I say I need wubba woof."

Mom: "I'm sorry. I'm not sure I'm hearing you correctly. Are you saying you need a rubber roof?"

Corey: "Yes. Wubba."

Mom: "OK, like a roof made out of rubber then?"

Corey: "Yes. You make dat?"

Mom: "Yyyyyyyeahhhhssss. Yes we can absolutely do that for you!" (My mother's company did not do rubber roofs. I don't even think my mother knew that was a possibility.)

Corey: "Oh my God, Mom, it's me. I'm fucking with you."

Mom: "Oh my God! You son of a bitch! You almost got me killed! I'm over here in traffic! Trying to talk on this phone. Make us some money! And this is the way you treat me!? I almost got hit by an eighteen wheeler! You would have been planning my funeral, you asshole! I can't believe you!"

This was one of the funniest moments of my life. Corey always joked around like that. One time, he pissed off his girlfriend so badly that she ran to the bus stop to go home. Corey was only wearing boxer shorts, and the nearest articles of clothing he could find were my niece's purple skinny jeans and red blouse. He threw those on and chased her down the street. She came back.

The day before Alexis and I left Pennsylvania for New Orleans, we had instructions to feed her boyfriend's boa constrictor. This means we had to go get mice. We got mice, but they had to wait in the car a bit because her brother was in Lil Abner that evening, and we stopped by to watch some of it. By the time we got back to the car, the mice had chewed their way through the box. I caught one, but he managed to bite my thumb. The other one ran loose in my car for the entire trip to New Orleans. He lived in there for another three weeks after we came home. I'd like to think he didn't have much to eat in there, but somehow he managed. I saw him periodically, but he always escaped back into the darkness when we'd try to catch him. One day, I was sitting in the parking lot at school eating some pizza, and I thought maybe the mouse would like some pizza too. He had become like a pet at this point. I placed the pizza box on the floorboard so that my mouse could have my leftovers. He came right over and started eating the pizza. I thought this was an opportune time to capture him so that I could let him go. I closed the pizza box abruptly while he was in it. He moved around for a second then stopped. I opened the box to check on him, and he was lifeless. I had accidentally closed the pizza box down on his neck, and it killed him. I cried for thirty fucking minutes before my microbiology exam because of that stupid mouse.

I had also taken a few road trips to North Carolina during college. My mom ended up buying a condo and moving there shortly after I started undergrad. The purpose of one specific trip was for me to drive down there to go car shopping with my mom. I was finally going to get rid of the Contour. I drove late into the night to get to North Carolina, so I slept in until about 10 the following morning. I was awakened by someone laying on their car horn outside. It was my mom. She was driving a blue convertible PT Cruiser. It was so cute! I immediately thought, "Oh my God! She went and got me a car! She must have been scoping it out for me!" I ran down the stairs to hop into my new ride. I said, "Is this my new car, Mom!?"

Marcina: "No. I decided to go and look because you gave me the idea. This is mine. I'm going to buy it for me. I never buy myself anything."

I'm sure there was some arguing at that point, but my mom did ultimately end up buying herself that car. I didn't get a car, and my ass was so chapped about it, that I packed up my luggage and went back to Pennsylvania that day. Several months later, when my mom came to Pennsylvania to visit, she bought window tint for my Ford Contour because she decided she felt bad about the whole deal. She bragged that it was the best, most expensive window tint they had. I accepted.

My mom came back to Pittsburgh to visit about every six months. I stayed at her house in Pittsburgh on the weekends so that I could tend bar. One such weekend, she came back with husband number seven. They came to the bar, and I didn't know it, but my boss kept serving number seven shots of Jim Beam. I had two rules as a bartender: Corey doesn't get more than eight beers in a night, and number seven doesn't get Jim Beam - period. If these two things occurred, they affected my life dramatically. When we got home, number seven fell asleep in the recliner. My mother and I slept on the only mattress in the house. My 18-year-old nephew slept on the floor with his sleeping bag. He stayed with me that summer. Number seven woke up and demanded that I let him sleep on the mattress. "No. I'm the girl. You're the drunk. You sleep on the chair". I know this sounds mean, but I had been sick of number seven for several years. He was a hypocrite. He always whooped Rachel's ass for having weed then took it from her to smoke it himself. He was a jerk. Rachel and I plotted to poison his coffee with *The Works* toilet bowl cleaner, too, but we ended up making homemade bombs with it instead.

Number seven did not like my response to his demands, so he decided to kick my little 19" TV that I bought for myself. I saw red. I jumped up and screamed at him. He grabbed my shoulders and kicked me in my shin. I cocked back my hand and punched him in his eye. My mother remained "asleep" during this whole episode, but she wasn't asleep. It would have been impossible to sleep through that. My nephew saw number seven kick me and stood up clenching his fists. He saw I was ok after I threw that punch, though. Number seven stormed out the door. My mom rolled over and asked what happened. I told her she knew exactly what had happened, and that she laid there and allowed it. I called the police. My mother asked me not to press charges. I told her to kiss my ass. The police had already picked up number seven a block away. They knew me well, not because I was a bad kid, but because Rachel was. I had pleaded with them several times to let her go free or to postpone her going to juvi. They listened to me most of the time. They asked me how number seven ended up with that "nice shiner". I smiled and told them I had no idea. Number seven spent the night in jail, and my mother was gone when I woke up. They had gone back to North Carolina. I didn't speak to her for a while.

Some months later, while studying Anatomy, I called my mother, frantic:

Me: "Mom! My anatomy book is WRONG!"

Mom: "What? What are you talking about?"

Me: "These idiots! I'm looking at these pictures of female genitalia, right?"

Mom: "Uh-huh."

Me: "Well, they're trying to say that women have a hole down there separate from their vaginas and their assholes!"

Mom: "Marlee, what in the hell are you talking about!? We do! We do have a separate hole! It's called a urethra! Tell me you're kidding! Come on, Marlee. You know that!"

Me: "What!? No we don't! Come on, Mom. Are you fucking with me!? Come on! I have to know this stuff, and it isn't funny if you're lying to me because I'll miss it on a test, and it'll be embarrassing!"

Mom: "No! What's embarrassing is raising a daughter who doesn't even know she doesn't piss out of her vagina!"

Me: "Mom! Seriously!?"

Mom: "Oh my God, Marlee, yes! For Christ's sake! Yes! Women pee out of a much smaller hole above their vaginas called a urethra. Jesus!"

Marlee: "I'm just not sure about this. I need a mirror. I'll call you back."

I was 21 years old and studying to be a physician when I discovered my own urethra. I would like to thank Frank Netter, who wrote *The Atlas of Human Anatomy,* for teaching me this. I would also like to blame my mother and my teachers for failing to teach me this at an appropriate age. In my defense, I went to Catholic elementary school, and we didn't have Sex Ed.

I didn't enjoy college the way other people say they do. I just remember counting the days until graduation. I started undergrad with hopes of becoming a physician. By the end of my college career, I decided I would be a physician assistant instead. I saw my academic advisor one day and told him I didn't want to devote the amount of time required to finish medical school. I told him I wouldn't be happy being a family doctor and that I would want to specialize, and that would take at least another eight years. After telling him how much I hated school, he recommended I become a physician assistant. He said it would be similar to being a physician but would require less schooling. He also said the salary was pretty decent. I was all-in. I knew I loved medicine, so I felt like there weren't many other options. I started applying to PA schools.

I took the GRE and applied to eight PA schools around the country. I scored interviews for three of them. I hated two of the schools I visited. One place made us write an essay about how we would be an asset as a physician assistant in a physician's office. It was then that I realized that I actually had no fucking clue what a physician assistant was. So, my essay consisted of a bunch of bullshit filler words with the phrase "I would be an asset as a physician assistant because I would help the doctor…" I literally had no idea what I would help a doctor do as a physician assistant. Needless to say, I was not accepted into that program. When I got home from there, I researched what a PA was so that I would be better prepared for my next interview. The next one was a roundtable interview where they had five faculty members rapid-fire questions at us and expected us to answer quickly and perfectly. I remember thinking they were all assholes and decided that even if I was accepted there, I would decline. I just didn't fit in there.

My last interview took place in Naples, Florida. It was 86 degrees in Naples that week, so I decided to go for a swim the day before my interview. It was January. When I got out of the pool and looked in the mirror, I realized my blonde hair had turned green from the pool water. I ran to the hotel office crying about how they had ruined my life because their pool turned my hair green and tomorrow was my PA school interview, which was the most important day of my life. Luckily the man at the desk was very obviously gay, so he had connections at Sally's Beauty Supply. He called his friend there and gave her a list of products I was coming to pick up. It was Sunday, and Sally's was about to close. He told them, "Melinda, hunnayyy! Isss Joshhhh! Listen hunnayy! I have a client here whose hair is three shades of peridot! She needs (insert product, insert product, and insert product!) She is leaving here right neow! Do NOT close that store! You wait for her to get there, you hear me?" I loved him. I picked up the products, and they got my hair to a blonde color with a green tint – a major improvement. The hotel owner even paid me back for the products.

The next morning, I showed up for my interview. The PA program would apparently be held in a trailer next to a small community college that year because the larger, state-of-the-art building was being constructed about fifteen miles up the highway and would not be complete until our class could no longer use it. They assured me the trailer was temporary and that the nice building would be ready by next year. I really didn't care about going to graduate school in a trailer and decided it was probably more my style anyway. I was really nervous for my interview there. I really liked Naples after being there for a day, and I could see myself living there. I really wanted to do well. The woman who met me at the front door was named Claudia. She was one of the sweetest people I had ever met. She told all the interviewees that we would do great and that everyone was very nice and not to worry. She told us she had our backs and to look at her if we felt nervous. She promised us she'd be there with us every step of the way. I talked with some of the other interviewees. They seemed much more nervous than I was, so that made me feel a little better.

It was my turn. Claudia called my name and held the door open for me, smiling. She was dressed to the nines and was wearing the cutest heels. She was about 60 years old. I remember thinking she was probably rich and wondered why she was working at all. "Take a deep breath. I'm here for you", said Claudia, this woman I'd just met fifteen minutes ago. I walked into the room, and there were three professors sitting at a table. "Fuck. Another roundtable interview", I thought. Claudia said, "Marlee, this is Professor Keena, Professor Coombs, and Doctor Vause. They're all very nice and are already very impressed by you. You're going to be fine". I smiled, told everyone hello and sat down.

Dr. Vause: "Marlee, we see you're coming here all the way from the great state of Pennsylvania!"

Me: "Yes Sir. I drove here two days ago. It's a beautiful place. Thanks so much for having me".

I tried to remain as professional as possible. They asked me a few questions about my hopes and dreams. I told them it was my dream to help people and how I've always had a fascination with medicine. I told them I wanted to treat the sickest of the sick someday. They asked me about my work history. I told them I hadn't done much except being a college student. I told them I was a waitress for two weeks but then promptly decided that wasn't the right business for me after a toddler reached onto my tray and scooped hot mashed potatoes onto himself. His mother yelled at me instead of him. I thought that was absurd, the little shit. Waitressing was just too much pressure for me. I told him that I had been a bartender for the past four years. The conversation quickly switched to them asking me how to make the best margaritas, long island iced teas, and any other drink they'd requested. Two minutes of the interview included questions and answers of substance. The remaining time was spent talking about booze. I tried to be as charming and funny as I could. I felt really comfortable around them, and they invited me to be myself. I walked out of that room knowing I was accepted. Claudia thought so, too. She told me they'd call me soon to let me know their final decision. Two weeks later, Claudia called congratulating me for my acceptance into PA school at Nova Southeastern University in Naples, Florida. I immediately accepted, hung up the phone, yelled and screamed, and did a somersault onto my bed.

"Religion is the opiate of the masses."

-Karl Marx

"I did masses of opiates religiously."

-Carrie Fisher

Mein Vater

I figured that since I was going to be moving away to Florida soon, if I was ever going to meet my real father, I should do it soon. I didn't intend to ever return to Pittsburgh except to visit family every few years, so I told my mom that I wanted to meet him. She said she knew the location of the home in which he last lived, but she wasn't sure he still lived there. I encouraged her to just drive by there and let me ask if he was still there or if the people living there may know him. I didn't have high expectations of finding him, but I felt obligated to at least try. I felt like if I hadn't tried, I would always have wondered what he was like. I at least wanted to be able to say I made an attempt to find out where I came from. On the following day, my mom drove me to the house where she last spent time with Pete. I knocked on the door, and an elderly man who spoke very broken English answered the door.

My Opa: "Hallo".

Me: "Hello. I am looking for Pete Popowicz. Do you know him, Sir?"

Opa: "Pete? Pete's at work.

Me: "Oh! OK! So he lives here? When does he get home from work?"

86

Opa: "He be here at 4:30". It was 2:30.

Me: "OK. Will you please tell him that a young lady came by looking for him and that I'll be back at 4:30 and to not leave?"

Opa: "Ja OK. Why you need Pete?"

Me: (My heart was pounding. I didn't know what to say.) "Sir, this is unbelievable, but my mother told me that Pete is my father. I am moving away to Florida within the next few weeks, and I wanted to meet him before I left. I promise that I am a normal person (my first lie to my grandfather), and I will be graduating from college soon. I would really love to just see him before I go. Please tell him to just stay here when he gets home from work."

Opa: "Ja. OK."

I expected a different reaction from my grandfather after telling him all this information. I later realized that he probably didn't understand a word I was saying because he spoke German and only very little English. He also had advanced Alzheimer's disease, so the fact that he even remembered to tell my father that I had stopped by would be a huge feat.

My mother and I decided to go get some lunch while waiting for my dad to come home from work. I wondered where he was working and what he did for a living. The only thing I had known about him was that he had a long struggle with heavy drugs and that he dropped out of college because he thought he was too smart to pay for educational institutions. I was so grateful to have found him but tried not to get too excited in fear that he would leave immediately after my grandfather had spoken with him about what was going on. I was worried that he wouldn't want to face me or that he wouldn't believe that I was his child. I wasn't even sure if I had believed it at that point. I couldn't even eat my lunch. At 4:35, we left to return to my father's house. I couldn't believe how close he'd lived to me for my whole life. I wondered if I'd ever come into contact with him. My mother told me that she ran into him at a Wendy's fast food joint when I was eight years old. She apparently saw him in line while I was sitting at a table, and she told him I was there and pointed me out. He said, "She's beautiful. She's a genius, isn't she? I told you she'd be a genius." I don't know if that's true, but I'd like to believe it is. It's a nice story.

We pulled up to my dad's driveway. I thought for sure he'd left or just never came home. His front door opened, and a man, about 5'11", who looked shockingly like Terry Bradshaw (except with really bad teeth and cataracts) emerged. He ran down the stairs, and I got out of the car. My mom stayed in the car with her window rolled down.

My dad: "Oh my God! Oh my God! I can't believe it! Oh my God! You're so beautiful. I can't believe it!! Marce (addressing my mom), can you believe this!? (Looking back at me) You are just...you know you're really German, right? I'm so sorry. I was so fucked up on shit n'at. I was on heroin for years, but now I'm clean. Been clean for sixteen years. My God. You are something".

He grabbed me up and hugged me without hesitation, and I knew I was his. I knew that this was the person I had come from. He was completely imperfect, and he was a mess. He was brutally honest. He was completely unafraid of humility. He told the whole truth, and he apologized for all his failures in just three sentences. I forgave him all at once, and I hugged him back. We both cried. I could hear my mother crying from inside the car. "Oh Pete!" she said, as she came out of the car with both arms out in front of her. I remember thinking she looked like she was walking like a zombie. She was being ridiculously dramatic. She hugged Pete. I don't remember much else about that day except that I finally felt like I belonged. I felt like I had found myself.

I made plans to meet up with Pete a week later. He took me to the public pool where he was apparently a stud because everyone knew him. He took me to a restaurant and paid for my meal. He told me to quit smoking as he puffed on his cigarette and lit mine. He told me all about his drug addiction and how he broke his parents' hearts by doing drugs and how he lost his brother to a heroin overdose. He said his brother's death was what finally convinced him to quit. He told me he had been sober for sixteen years and decided to make a career of being a drug counselor at the local methadone clinic. He had been working there ever since. I told him I was proud of him, and it was OK that he wasn't around. He told me, "It looks like your mother did a great job with you though!" "Yeah", I said, smiling. "I'm making it OK. I graduate from college next week. I'd like for you to be there if you can swing it. I'm moving to Florida to be a physician assistant. It seems like a cool gig." I tried to talk extra cool because my dad was super cool. My mom told me he was the most popular, coolest guy she'd ever met. She said everyone loved him and everyone knew him. He made friends everywhere he went. She said he had the greatest personality, and she told me that's where I got it from. She said he was witty and extremely smart. He told me he tried his hand at college, but that he was a genius, so college was boring for him, so he moved to California to do drugs instead. Much later in my life, I was in a bar in Brookline, Pennsylvania (where my dad grew up and lived), and I told a guy I was Pete's daughter. He looked at me in awe and told me my dad was the coolest guy who'd ever lived. He also told me that my dad was responsible for a huge drug smuggling operation from California to Pittsburgh back in the '70s that involved a hijacked plane. "It was a different time then", both he and my dad said. "Everyone was doing it." I could totally see my dad being just like Johnny Depp in the movie *Blow*. It made perfect sense.

My dad came to my college graduation. I remember him describing the day in awe. "It's amazing to see so many young people making achievements. I missed out on that part of life. It's just amazing to see hundreds of kids just doing right, ya know. And the sun was aht (out). And the clouds were beautiful. It was like something aht of a movie watching you up there, kid". To me it was normal. I was destined to grow up, go to college, have a career, and *do right*. But I realized it doesn't happen that way for everyone. In fact, it doesn't happen that way for most people.

We decided to have a celebratory dinner in honor of my graduation, so we went to Eat 'N' Park. For those of you who don't know, Eat 'N' Park isn't exactly a "celebratory dinner" kind of place, but that's OK. Eat 'N' Park is like a ghetto Denny's. I asked my dad to make the hour-long trip back to Pittsburgh with me, but my mom quickly grabbed his arm and said, "No. Pete and I have lots of catching up to do! You guys go ahead!" I wanted to scream at her, but I also wanted to remain calm around Pete, so I left in my own car. The dinner was nice, except that I didn't even get to talk to my dad because my mother insisted they have their own table away from the rest of us. I have no idea what they talked about, but I know she somehow talked him into paying for all of our meals. I was embarrassed about that.

Three days after my graduation from college, I left for Florida to start my graduate school program. It was an eighteen hour drive. My mom decided to make the trek in a separate vehicle with me so that we could have more space. By this time, I had acquired more than just a papasan chair, so I obliged. We loaded up the Contour and her truck, but my mom had one surprise. She had convinced herself that we needed an extra hand (though we certainly didn't), so we would be bringing Uncle Al along with us. Al was a skinny, older, frail, alcoholic version of Jeff Bridges. I could have bench pressed Uncle Al easily. You could see the neon yellow in his eyes and smell the booze on Uncle Al from ten yards away. I was not sure what kind of help he was going to be for me, but I'm sure my mom found him rather resourceful. Five years prior, when I was in high school, I walked down the stairs of my childhood home to find my mom giving Uncle Al a blowie on the couch at 6:00 in the evening, which I thought was a bizarre time of day for a BJ in the living room while your grown children are at home, but whatever.

I needed my mom's help, and I figured I could at least get some free meals out of her on the way there, so I agreed that Uncle Al could come along. Pollo, the now-healed, previously burned chinchilla, would be my riding buddy. I had sold Quesadilla because someone offered me $200 for her. Our bond was just not as strong. It was a pretty smooth trip until ¾ of a mile from our final exit in Naples. It was prom night in that area, and there was a terrible car accident just eight cars ahead of us. Traffic was halted for hours, and the medical chopper landed right on the highway. Hundreds of young kids were running from their cars in traffic to see if their friends were involved. It turned out, they were. I read in the local paper that two high school kids were killed in that accident on their prom night while driving under the influence of alcohol. It was a terrible situation, and it was talked about in the town for weeks.

We spent the next few days unloading my stuff, checking out the area, and waiting for my roommates to arrive. Al spent the next few days drinking vodka and pissing on our beautifully landscaped plants in the front yard. I managed to get my mom to buy me some frozen Jimmy Dean breakfast sandwiches and a set of plastic Tupperware drawers for my clothes so I could make it through the next 2½ years of my life. I think she felt guilty about bringing Al along because he consistently made an ass of himself. We went to Sam's club, and he managed to get away from us. We later found him sleeping on the display set of outdoor furniture. My roommate Ashley arrived with her family from Minnesota. She was the cutest, sweetest thing I had ever seen, and her family was very nice. When we first met, she said to me, "So wonderful to meet you in person! Hey! Did you guys know there is a guy sleeping in the passenger's seat of a truck out front? His legs are hanging out the window, and he's snoring.

91

It's SO funny! You should go look!" I said, "No way! That's so funny! What an idiot!" and gave my mom the death stare. It was Al. She read my mind. They were leaving in the morning whether they liked it or not.

Ashley was precious, and her family was very wealthy. Lindsay, my other roommate, showed up shortly after with her family, also very wealthy. They managed not to notice the drunk guy snoring with his legs out of the truck window, or at least they were nice enough not to mention it. Lindsay was blonde and thin and gorgeous. I chose the room with the sliding door to the backyard so I could go out there and smoke. Ashley brokered the real estate deal, so she got the room with the jetted tub and separate shower. Lindsay was just grateful to be there (plus she showed up last), so she just took what was left.

PA school was a blast! I had never enjoyed school so much. I was finally learning what I wanted to be learning. The professors were cool. They talked to us like we were normal human beings. There were people in my class who were old enough to be my parents. Everyone was respected. Shortly after we started, I scoped out a guy who sat across the room. He had long, brown hair and gauged earrings. I thought he was mysterious. I didn't talk to him much, though. I was still dating Chris. That changed abruptly when Chris came to Florida for a visit, got super drunk, and vomited in my new friend's van. Then it was over. I sent him back to Pittsburgh single, although I think he was already dating someone else there, so he was fine. We'll call this mysterious man Derek.

Derek and his roommates hosted a party at their house one night. I swam in their pool, ate their food, and danced to their music. It was a great party. I remember looking over and seeing mysterious Derek sitting alone, drinking a beer, and popping tramadol. I had to have him. I know what you're saying...three red flags in one sentence. Don't ask me why, but I was attracted to him. Maybe it was the earrings. Maybe it was the "bad boy" thing. I finally talked to him. He told me I was "interesting". He mentioned he had a girlfriend back in Alabama. I ignored that and considered it a non-issue. More red flags. Derek and I started hanging out more and more and eventually fell for each other. He broke up with his girlfriend to date me then cheated on me with her twice. Each time he cheated, he cried to me about how he was sorry and told me he'd never do it again. He was obnoxious when he drank, which was all the time. He was disrespectful toward me lots of the time, and I knew I shouldn't have been offering my time to him. We broke up and got back together a lot. We argued all the time. I'm sure our friends were sick of it. We had the exact same friends, which made our arguments awkward for everyone. Eventually, we grew to understand each other and became sure that we wanted to be together for some reason. He cut back on drinking. I cut back on being nuts about it. Then he'd drink, and I would go nuts. This continued for many years.

I loved the clinical part of my training to become a physician assistant. The classroom part wasn't so fun, but it was much better than undergrad. Eventually our class discovered Google Chat. All the "cool" people in class suddenly created Gmail accounts, and almost all the students sent messages to each other all day during class. That was a blast! That's how most of us made it through the didactic year of PA school. We all vowed to dedicate our master's degrees to G chat. At the end of that year, our professors prepared us to actually see clinical patients for the next year. They decided the best way to do this was to send us to assisted living facilities. We were asked to take medical histories and perform routine physical examinations on some of the residents. Most of us were really excited about actually laying our hands on human patients. The only other time we could do this was when the school hired surrogates to come to our building so that we could practice genital exams. This is completely normal in medical education, and people get paid big bucks for it, so the surrogates are easy to find. My pelvic exam went fine. The lady was actually very helpful. She knew her way around her vagina. She told us, "No you're not there yet. Move left. There you go. You see it now?" It was awkward, but it was also a great learning experience.

My male genital exam wasn't such a great learning experience, but it was definitely awkward. Before we did the actual exam, we had to take a history on the guy. All the other students asked questions like, "Do you have any specific complaints today? What is your medical history? Do you smoke?" But I knew we were there for a genital exam, and I wasn't afraid, so I asked him straight-up, "Are you sexually active". Apparently it takes people years to feel comfortable asking this question. It was pretty second nature to me. I would not have asked if I had known this guy was going to respond, "I don't know. Depends. What are you doing later!?" I didn't know he was preparing me for real-life medicine. I still get this exact response nowadays. We laughed it off and went on with our exams, which consisted of feeling all over his penis and scrotum and then sticking a finger in his ass. I was in the room when my partner did his rectal exam. The surrogate looked at me and smiled during the exam. I started to think this guy was a real creeper. It was my turn. I examined his penis, which showed to have a little premature ejaculate issue. I did my rectal exam and got out of there as quickly as I could. That night, the guy was arrested for exhibitionism in his hotel. He flashed the maid his wiener. Creeper. I was right.

We drove to the assisted living facility to take histories and do exams on old, demented people. Don't get me wrong. I love old, demented people, but for the purposes of taking a history on them, they are fucking useless. I was finally going to be able to talk to a human being about her medical ailments. I was excited. I had high expectations. Imagine my disappointment when I asked, "Mrs. Lovett, tell me about your past medical history" and Mrs. Lovett responded, "The damn fish is green! They tried to tell me it's orange, but I don't believe them! It's GREEN!" "Mrs. Lovett, I'm trying to ask you about your medical history, like any prior medical problems that you have or had". "What time is lunch? I'm starving. Are you cooking my lunch!? Bring me my goddamn lunch!" You see, they don't tell you you're not going to get information from these people. It took me months to learn that sometimes people won't give you shit for information, and you just have to figure it out for yourself or not figure it out at all – which is more likely the case. So, on all those trips to the assisted living facilities, I just did crafts with the old people and listened to their hearts and lungs. I still learned from them. I learned that ignorance is bliss, and that sometimes the only "medicine" people need is for you to sit and do crafts and tell jokes with them. And sometimes people are just happy to have you around because they don't have anybody else. And it's cool for you to be there for them, even if they are demanding for you to drop everything and make them a fucking sandwich. Maybe that's what our professors were trying to teach us by sending us there.

My clinical year of PA school was much better. We had a little time to do other things like go to the beach or to the club. I remember being scared shitless about my first rotation because they decided to put me with the preceptor who was known to be the biggest jerk of all of them. He was a surgeon – a very good surgeon, which meant he was like a god in his hospitals. During my first surgery, on my first day, I nearly passed out. I didn't feel queasy or anything, and the procedure was almost over. I thought it was super cool. Then I got hot and dizzy and almost fell. He told me I'd never make it in medicine because of that. I didn't like that comment, so the following morning, I woke up at 3:00 a.m. to be at the hospital by 4:30. I asked the nurses which patients Dr. Kokal would be responsible for seeing. I examined all of those patients and had progress notes written on all of them before he got there. He took me out to lunch that day and offered me a job by the end of that rotation. He used to page me throughout the hospital as "Myrtle". He called me Myrtle because he could never initially remember my name. The nurses all said he called me that because he liked me and that he had never treated a student so well. It was cool being accepted amongst such talented people. People loved him. They respected him.

Lots of them were scared of him, but I liked the ones who stood up to him. He needed it sometimes. And he didn't really respect me until I stood up to him a couple of times, too. I used to tell him off in the operating room all the time. And I made him a CD with rap songs on it so we could listen to it during our long surgeries, and one day he shook his butt with me to the song *Low* by Flo Rida. You know "Apple bottom jeans. Boots with the fur." I was sick of that boring crap he listened to in there. He needed a little flavor in his life. Three weeks after he told me I'd never make it in medicine, I diagnosed my first case of terminal cancer with that man.

A 35 year old guy walked in to our office for a "growth" on his chest. He was so handsome. He took his shirt off, and we knew what it was immediately. "Melanoma", the doctor said. "What's that?" asked the patient.

Doc: "It's cancer. And it looks bad. I'm going to shoot it to you straight. People die from this. And it looks bad. Really bad. How long has it been there?"

Patient: "Four years maybe. It's been growing. I was too afraid to get it checked out. My wife finally made me come in here."

Doc: "Well I've never seen one this size that hasn't metastasized. That means it's likely it has spread to other parts of your body. And four years is a very long time for a melanoma to continue to grow. I'm going to order a PET scan to see if we've got anything else going on. Bring your wife to your next appointment."

It turns out the guy had metastatic cancer to the lymph nodes, lung, liver, and brain. He met with oncology, but they collectively decided to not undergo treatments such as surgery or chemotherapy. The man died shortly after at the age of 36. He thanked my doctor for being so honest about his initial diagnosis. He and his wife had apparently been having problems, but it allowed them enough time to fix things amongst them and their children before he died. He hugged us both and thanked us profusely. I never thought a person would thank someone for a terminal cancer diagnosis, but I have seen it many times since. After working with this physician and making other like diagnoses, I decided to adopt that kind of practice. People want to know the whole truth about their illnesses. They don't want a candy coating. I remember thinking it was odd that a young man with a family would wait four years to finally go see a doctor for something he knew was wrong. I have learned that it happens quite often in medicine. I have learned not to judge people for it. Everyone has their own personal fears, and we react differently when faced with them. I am glad this man ultimately decided to come in to see us. He taught me much more than he could ever have known.

I maintained contact with my dad while I was in Florida. I even visited with him once when I made a trip to Pittsburgh for a short break. I had conversations with my grandfather – in German this time. He never remembered me because of the Alzheimer's, but he was excited to find out he had another granddaughter every time I told him. That made it more fun. My father and I talked on the phone about every two weeks. I bought him a Father's Day gift. That was really cool for me. It was something I never thought I'd be able to do. He really appreciated it. I'm sure he never thought he'd get a Father's Day gift from a daughter. I remember ending one phone conversation with my dad saying, "OK, I'll talk to you in a few. Love you!" He responded similarly, but he sounded frail or sad. It sounded like he was crying. I hung up anyway. I didn't want to hurt his pride and ask if he was crying. I thought maybe he just thought it was nice to say he loved me or to hear me say it to him, but we said it often at that point, so I didn't know what it was about. I was sure he was crying. A week later, I was sitting on my bed studying, and I received a phone call from my brother Corey's father. "Marlee, honey. I have something to tell you. Are you sitting down?"

Me: "Yeah. I'm studying. What's up?"

Corey's dad: "OK I'm just going to say it, OK?"

Me: "Yeah. Ok then! Say it. What's up?"

Corey's dad: "Petey's dead, honey. I was reading the paper today and saw his obituary. It says he'd been fighting a short battle with lung cancer, and he died in the hospital a few days ago from pneumonia."

Me: (Holy fuck! Try and keep it together.) "Aw man. That sucks so bad. Is there a funeral?"

Corey's dad: "It says they aren't doing anything formal. They're just going to have a mass for him, and it's tomorrow. I don't think that gives you enough time to get here. I'm sorry honey. If I had known, I would have called you sooner."

Me: "It's OK. Thanks for letting me know."

Corey's dad: "Are you OK?"

Me: "Yeah. I'm OK. I didn't know him that long. It was cool to get to know him. I'll be fine. Thanks again."

Corey's dad: "OK. I'm here for you."

Me: "I know. Thanks."

As soon as I hung up the phone, I screamed. I screamed, "NO!" And it must have been a gut-wrenching scream because Lindsay ran into my room and grabbed my forearms and asked me what was wrong. I fell to the floor and told her what had happened. She started crying and told me she was sorry. I felt bad about her crying, so I stopped. I told her it would be OK and that I didn't know him that long but that it was just bizarre because I knew he started crying at the end of our conversation the other day. Maybe he wanted to tell me he was sick but didn't want to worry me. Maybe he knew that would be the last time we spoke. Maybe he had something more to say, but I just hung up because I was trying to protect his pride. I convinced Lindsay I would be fine, so she left my room. I sat and just thought. I thought about all of the things I didn't get to ask him. I thought about how I wouldn't even be able to be there for his funeral mass and burial. I thought about how no one else in the family knew me except for my Opa, and he would never remember I existed. I thought about how that would be the last connection I would have with that part of my family, and I would never know them. I was grateful to have been able to know my real father, even if it was just for a short while.

"With regard to healing the sick, I will devise and order for them the best diet, according to my judgment and means; and I will take care that they suffer no hurt or damage. Nor shall any man's entreaty prevail upon me to administer poison to anyone; neither will I counsel any man to do so... Further, I will comport myself and use my knowledge in a godly manner... If I faithfully observe this oath, may I thrive and prosper in my fortune and profession, and live in the estimation of posterity; or on breach thereof, may the reverse be my fate!"

-The Hippocratic Oath

Trauma Drama

It was 0700 on the first day of my emergency medicine rotation. I walked through the doors of the emergency department to find my preceptor. I introduced myself, and he said, "Good! CPR in progress. Room 17. Go do some compressions." Holy shit. Already!? What are the chances of there being a newly dead guy in the room the second I walk in on my first fucking day? I wasn't prepared for this. I figured they would ease me into it by first letting me see a patient with a toothache, then maybe a back pain, then maybe a simple pneumonia and go from there. No. I get the dead guy! I wanted to tell the doctor that I actually had come to the wrong place and that I think I still had one more day in internal medicine upstairs, but I didn't. I was scared. You know what I've since learned about the patient who is the dead guy? He can't possibly get any worse. You'll have to excuse my humor about emergency medicine. All people in emergency medicine have an odd sense of humor, and it's necessary to make it through some days.

The patient was in cardiac arrest. "Code blue". Asystole. "Flat-lined". No pulse, no respirations, and no blood pressure. He had been down for about fifteen minutes. He was chronically ill. He was old and thin and had no teeth. He had been battling lung cancer with some kind of metastasis for a long time. When I walked in, the respiratory therapist was attempting to supply oxygen to him by holding a mask tightly over his mouth and squeezing a bag full of air. It wasn't working, though, because the guy had no teeth. His lips just flapped, and no air went into his mouth. Maybe he got some through his nose. The doctor had gathered his tools and was able to put a tube in the patient's mouth, advance it into his throat then lungs so he could better ventilate him. He connected the bag full of air to the tube in the lungs, and the respiratory therapist squeezed every few seconds. While all of this was going on, a stocky, sweaty paramedic pushed forcefully and rhythmically on the patient's chest. I remember hearing a "pop", and everyone else ignored it. It made me cringe because I knew it was the man's ribs cracking. Two nurses tried to get IV access, one In each arm. They weren't successful on the first try, so one of the techs brought over a little leather kit and unzipped it. A nurse drilled a big needle into the patient's lower leg with a handheld machine and started some IV fluids. I remember nurses and the doctor yelling out the names of different drugs and always asking, "How long has it been since we gave epi?" "Three minutes!" "OK. More epi! Now!" It was chaos, but it was organized chaos. The paramedic said he had to switch out because he was getting tired, and everyone looked at me. Everyone else was busy doing more important things, and I was just standing there shitting my pants. I wanted to just wave at everybody, nod, give them a "thumbs up" put my head down and slowly back out of the room and disappear, but I knew I had a job to do. I took a deep breath, jumped on the stool, and gave the best chest compressions I could. No one paid attention to me. I guess they just figured I had extensive training in this sort of thing, and I would be fine. This was not true. We spent like twenty minutes on this section in school, and I was tired the day we learned it. I wanted some feedback because I remember thinking that was a pretty important job and someone should probably be telling me if I was fucking it up. This guy was going to die if I didn't do great compressions. "Die!? Oh my God!" I felt faint. All of this responsibility was on my shoulders. I looked at the man, eyes wide open. Lifeless. Toothless. A tube surrounded in vomit hanging out of his mouth. I looked at this thin, broken chest that I was forcefully, repetitively pushing down on. The doctor said, "Good compressions." That was it! I was going to save this guy's life with these good compressions! "I am the best fucking chest compressor ever! Come on, old guy. Live! Man, I'm tired. My arms hurt. I'm hungry. No! Save the dead guy, Marlee. I can't. I'm too tired. I think I forgot to eat breakfast." "I need to switch", I yelled. The paramedic was already standing behind me waiting for me to give up. "Good job", he said as he jumped on the stool with me. They called that man's time of death shortly after. We offered a moment of silence for the deceased. We didn't save the dead guy, but we didn't make him any worse.

I walked out of the room not knowing what I felt. I felt sorry for the old man and for his family. I imagined he had many children and grandchildren and that they were waiting in the family room for us to come out and tell them that he miraculously turned around, and he would welcome them with hugs and kisses soon. But then I thought about how the guy looked like he was 90, and he spent the last few years as a very sick person. I thought that 90 was probably a good time to go. "Better 90 than 36", I thought. Then, I thought about what I had just been involved in, and initially I wanted to go splash water on my face or ask someone to pinch me. Then, I felt proud to have been involved in something so important, even though the outcome was not what we had hoped for. It was the biggest adrenaline rush I had ever had, and I was hooked.

"Hey, Marlee! How'd it go?" asked the doctor. "Well...he died. But I was told I did good compressions." "Eh. He was dead already, right? You gave your best effort. That's all you can do. There's a patient who sounds like an acute CHF (congestive heart failure) in room six. You want it?" I just watched a man die. I cannot do work right now! I need to go have diarrhea or something. You don't know what I just went through! And I'm supposed to just pick up another chart and go look another man in his face and pretend nothing ever happened!? "Yeah, sure. I'll take it. Where's the chart?" In PA school, they taught us a very valuable lesson. "Fake it 'til you make it", they said. And it's true. There are going to be things that you don't want to do, things you're not comfortable doing. But eventually you have to get in there and do it, so make it sooner than later. Ask your docs and colleagues all the questions in the world, but don't look dumb in front of a patient. Tell them you have a phone call and go Google that shit they just asked you about. It's not about knowing all the information. That's impossible. It's about knowing where to find the right information and being educated enough to decipher what's important and what's truth versus what's not.

I absolutely loved my emergency medicine rotation. After trying out other specialties, I decided this is where I would stay. I couldn't work anywhere else, especially obstetrics. I delivered a baby once, and it was a beautiful experience: beautiful mother, beautiful father, healthy, beautiful baby. Easy delivery. Momma was a pro and had realistic expectations of what her delivery should be like. It was an amazing experience. The parents hugged and kissed and held their new son and thanked each other and thanked us for their new gift. I still think childbirth is a miracle. Delivering babies is just not for me. But I do see more vaginas than I had ever expected in the ER.

I once pulled an eight ball of cocaine out of a woman's vagina. This story will end here because that one sentence should be entertaining enough. Savages.

Another reason I don't belong in OB is because I actually did pass out while holding a retractor in a woman's abdomen during a C-section. I was unconscious, lying on the ground in the operating room. I didn't eat breakfast that day, and the surgeon thought it would be funny to throw some meconium at me as a joke. Meconium is essentially a baby's first turd. It is not a joke, and it should not be thrown around in an operating room because people may pass out because of it! Everyone in medicine passes out in a surgery at some point. It's another thing they don't tell you while you're in school, so you feel like a complete ass when you're out in the field and it happens. I have since had several students pass out in the ER while watching things. One time, a guy cut off four of his fingers with a saw. We had to do a nerve block on him for pain relief because the pain meds were not effective. I had an excellent student at the time. She was standing beside me watching the nerve block, and the next thing I knew, she was leaning hard against me. At first I thought she was trying to snuggle with me, but I looked at her, and her eyes were in the back of her head. The only thing holding her up was my shoulder. I held her there and told my tech to get a chair and put it behind her. The patient didn't even know she had passed out because we were slick about it. She came-to immediately after, as is what usually happens. "I'm so sorry", she said. "It happens to everyone. No worries! You're still a rock star, girl!" I failed her because of that. I'm kidding. She was one of my favorite students.

We had a pharmacy student who felt faint while watching open heart surgery, so he decided it would be a good idea to go and get a Coca Cola to feel better. Pharmacy students don't belong in open heart surgeries. They found him at the bottom of the staircase bleeding from his mouth and nose. His nose was fractured, and he had a nasty laceration across his midface. He had a hole in his chin and was missing most of his front teeth. When I pulled out his lower lip, I could see bony fragments in his mandible. He was handsome otherwise. I fixed him up the best I could, but he ultimately had to have facial reconstructive surgery. If you feel faint, just sit down. Don't go get a soda.

PA school was coming to a close. I had many job offers in Florida, but I was holding out for Derek to figure out what he was going to do with his life. He decided that he wanted to move back to Alabama and take over his parents' medical practice. He told me I could come with him. He didn't ask me to come. He just kind of said I could come along if I'd like. I really didn't have anything else going on, so I decided to try to get an ER rotation in Alabama as my last elective rotation. Derek went to Alabama for his last rotation, so I was able to stay with him at his parents' house. They knew me by then and were learning to pretend they liked me for his sake. I wasn't their kind of person. They were rich and thought they were "cultured". I remember always wanting to drop them off in the projects for a night just to see what would happen. I had tattoos and bleach blonde hair. I talked like a "Yankee" because I am one. I wore lots of gold jewelry because at that point I was proud of what I had acquired and wore every piece of jewelry I owned at the same time. Plus, I was (am) half 'hood because that's where I came from. I figured I could put on a good enough show to stay in their mansion for a month. After all, I was just about to graduate with a master's degree, so that should have been good enough.

At one point a few months later, Derek's mother came to pick me up because we were all going golfing that day. I put on my longest shorts and a polo shirt, thinking that was golf-appropriate attire but knowing damn well I did not belong on a fucking golf course. I got in her car and she said, "We need to get you some new clothes. This isn't Miami, you know!" I wanted to punch her in the throat because I had just lived pretty much in Miami for two years. This was the least slutty summer outfit I owned. I did take her up on her offer for her to buy me clothes later, though. I figured I was a professional at that point and would need to play the part a little. Plus, I had never passed up the opportunity to spend someone else's money if they were willing to spend it.

I scored an ER rotation in Decatur, Alabama because a doctor there was nice enough to respond to my thirty phone calls. Persistence is key. Or annoyance. Either way, it worked. I think this guy was ultimately glad he accepted me as a student because he eventually offered me a job. He was a phenomenal ER doctor. Sometimes he got mad and acted like a sissy, though. I learned that the nurses had a stash of candy bars for this exact reason. If he was pissed, all you had to do was offer him a Snickers, and he was fine. It worked every time. It's funny how nurses learn how to calm doctors down, or make them feel stupid, or ruin their lives. Nurses are not people to mess with. This is valuable information. My mother, a nurse herself, had always told me that your nurses will make or break your career in medicine. I have found this to be true. Nurses oversee everything that happens in the facilities in which they work. Doctors, physician assistants, nurse practitioners, and administrators have fake power. Nurses are the bosses. Remember that when you're the patient. They choose the sizes of your needles and your Foley catheters. Be nice to them.

I accepted the job in Alabama because Derek finally did say he wanted me to be there with him. I figured he'd gotten all his cheating and treating me badly out of his system, and we were going to actually be able to end up together. Our families came to Florida to celebrate our graduation with us. We purchased hotel rooms right on the beach in Fort Lauderdale, Florida. It was a good time. It was the one time I was able to see Derek's mother stop being so damn judgmental and just be a normal human being. This only happened because my sister Rachel got her drunk on some stuff that she said only had 3% alcohol in it, but it actually had way more. It tasted like juice, though, so Derek's mom believed her.

I guess I should better describe Rachel at this point. Rachel had been in and out of juvenile detention centers since she was 14. She also realized that she was gay when she was about that age, too, but she thought she'd try it out with boys just in case. Plus, it wasn't socially acceptable to just be yourself at that time. She aspired to be a famous rapper, and she's actually really good at it. She had a couple suicide attempts, including one where she woke me up in the middle of the night to tell me she had just taken all of her antidepressants at once. I put my finger in her throat and made her vomit to get rid of them. She ended up being OK. She was a talented con artist by the time I graduated from PA school.

Rachel took one look at Derek's mother and decided she was going to make her loosen up. Derek's mom was eating out of the palm of her hand by the end of the night. She was drunk, giggling and hiccupping, walking off-balance, swearing. It was a big deal. She made an ass of herself, and that was Rachel's master plan. And I am eternally grateful for her for that night.

Life in Alabama was nice. I lived rent-free in a mansion, but it meant that I'd have to walk around in long slacks and a turtleneck with a vest most of the time for my outfit to be deemed appropriate attire. I got free meals, so it was worth it. I didn't start working for a few months due to a delay in licensing. I was busy trying to get Derek's license in order so that he could take over the medical practice for his parents, so I postponed attempting to get my own. He wasn't really good at taking care of himself. I remember him telling me that he showed up to his PA school interview hungover from the night before. He didn't take things very seriously. He procrastinated a lot. He went to work about two months before me which meant he'd have to support me. I had my job lined up, so that was comforting. I really hated feeling like someone was taking care of me. He hated it more. We bought our own house shortly after I started bitching every day about living with his parents. The free food was no longer worth it, so you know it had to be bad. I was grateful for them welcoming me into their home, but there's only so much judgment and daily harassment a person can take. Dinner table discussions consisted of politics and racism. I'm not racist. They tried to say they weren't either. I have mixed feelings about politics. I don't belong in any category, but if I had to choose, I'd say I'm closest to libertarian. They were extremely conservative. Most of my friends were black or gay. We had absolutely nothing in common.

Derek and I bought a beautiful house on the other side of town but still close to Derek's parents. We had to fix it up a little, so I learned how to do that. Derek was also into flipping and selling houses, so I learned a lot. We had eventually acquired eight rental houses and flipped three. Living with a guy who is trying to run three businesses sucks, especially if he spends his off days getting drunk and taking Xanax and Adderall – prescription drugs with two opposite effects. It's like living with a man who is purposely making himself bipolar. I remember going to bed one night, sleeping soundly, and my phone rang at 3 a.m. I had an uncomfortable feeling because no one calls me in the middle of the night unless something bad happened. I looked at my phone. It was Rachel.

Me: "Hey. What's up? You OK?"

Rachel: (Sobbing, barely able to speak) "Corey's dead!"

Me: "What!? What the FUCK!" I jumped out of bed. "What is going on!? Where are you? Corey our brother!?"

Rachel: "He spent the night at his new girlfriend's house. I'm watching the paramedics. Oh my God! They're bringing him out covered-up on a stretcher now. Our brother's dead!"

Me: "Oh my God! What happened?"

Rachel: "We don't know. No one knows. Mom is inside the house. I'm in her truck. Oh my God I want to die!"

I wanted to die, too. But I couldn't tell Rachel that. I had to be strong and try and stay calm for her. I was the only person she could talk to right then, and she was confiding in me. I knew I couldn't confide in her because she wasn't strong enough for that.

Rachel: "Mom's coming back. I have to go. I'll call you right back. I love you so much."

Me: "Oh my God, Rachel. I'm so sorry. Call me right back. I love you."

I stood there for a minute. It didn't feel real. Corey was 29 and relatively healthy. Two years prior, after a night of heavy drinking, Corey attempted to crawl over the railing to get to the front porch of my mom's condo in North Carolina. It was something we all did all the time because she always locked the door to the patio but never locked the sliding glass door to get into the house. His foot slipped, and he fell forty feet to the concrete below. My mom said she heard a loud bang, and it woke her from her sleep. She saw Corey on the ground below her condo bleeding from his head. She ran down the stairs and held him. He was unconscious but still breathing. He had multiple terrible skull and pelvic fractures and an intracranial hemorrhage. After several months of hospitalization, he ended up being alright, but from then on, he took heavy pain medications several times daily. He never stopped taking those medications. He changed a little after his brain injury. He was never quite as nice. I didn't speak to him as much after his accident. I didn't really speak to him at all for the last year of his life. Our relationship had become toxic. I didn't agree with his lifestyle, and he didn't care to hear about it. He had become an alcoholic and a prescription drug addict. I thought it was better to love him from afar. Even now, after he's gone, I don't think it could have happened any other way. I wish I had a better relationship with him, but drugs make people inconsistent. They come in and out of your life randomly. Sometimes people on drugs are wonderful, and sometimes they're absolutely unbearable, no matter how much you love them. Corey and Tarah, my best friend, had a baby together a few years prior. Corey was inconsistent in his son's life, too. He also has a daughter from a previous relationship, and he wasn't any better there. He used to say he hated himself and wished he would die. I wished it hadn't happened. He was the life of the party. He never took anything seriously. He was the funniest person in the world. He could have done anything he ever wanted, but he didn't believe in himself. He had always been told by his father that he would never amount to anything, and he believed it.

I shook Derek to wake him up.

Me: "Hun, I need someone."

Derek: "What's going on?"

Me: "Rachel just called me. She said they just pronounced Corey dead."

Derek: "Your brother Corey?"

Me: "Yeah."

Derek: "The one you don't like?"

Derek never bothered to remember my brother's names. I wasn't terribly close with any of them, and he never talked to them, so I guess it just wasn't important to him.

Me: (What the fuck is wrong with you? Who says that?) "The one I don't get along well with, yeah."

Derek: "Well I'm sorry baby, but I have work in the morning. Would it be OK if I slept? I'm really sorry."

Me: (You son of a bitch!) "I'm going to go call Tarah."

I got ahold of Tarah a few hours later. Her phone was turned off, and I had to call her house and wake up her mother. I felt terrible about doing that, but Tarah's mother is essentially my mother. She cried and apologized and told Tarah to get on the phone.

Tarah: (Knowing I would never call her house that late) "What's wrong?"

Me: "Rachel called me and told me Corey was pronounced dead after sleeping at his girlfriend's house last night."

She wanted to know what happened. How could that happen? We all wanted to know. No one could believe it. The autopsy report said he died of pneumonia. I'm sure it was a combination of that and his prescribed medications causing some respiratory failure when he was already sick. I loved my brother. I thought the world of him. I hope he knew that as he was leaving this world.

"Tragedies will always be found in the things we love. And if we are not willing to see the beauty in losing something that means the world to us, then imagine how terrible it will be to live for them.

We must always welcome the end of all things. For sometimes, knowing nothing lasts forever is the only way we can learn to fall in love with all the moments and all the people that are meant to take our breath away."

R.M. Drake

The Bible Belt

Although it was not terribly long ago, my time spent in Alabama is sort of a blur for me. My relationship with Derek was difficult from the start, and it stayed that way. There was probably never more than a one-month period when we didn't have a huge fight. We were two totally different people who thought we were in love. I didn't agree with some of his choices, and he thought I was too difficult. We kept hoping that one day it would change.

Things were going very well with my career. I was promoted to being the boss of all of the physician assistants and nurse practitioners in the ER. It was a compliment because I was very young. People had always told me I was a "natural" in the ER. I just knew that I loved it and couldn't see myself doing anything any different. I picked up more shifts at work since my relationship was failing miserably. I worked nearly every day, and I worked at lots of different places. I learned how to get along with all types of people and how to perform different functions at different facilities. I saw a lot, good and bad.

I remember seeing a sixteen year old girl with muscular dystrophy who came in with a cough for two weeks. She was in the fast-track, so we figured she wasn't a real emergency. She had a little developmental delay, but she seemed pretty bright. She said it was only a mild cough, and it only bothered her a little. She said she had something similar six months prior, and she took some antibiotics, and it went away. She thought she needed more antibiotics. Her lungs sounded normal. She looked great. So I told her I would get her a prescription, and she'd be on her way. I stepped just outside her door, and a strange feeling washed over me. I felt like something was wrong. I have had this feeling many more times in my career, and I cannot explain where it comes from, but it is real, and it usually means something is terribly wrong. I walked back in her room and said, "I'm sorry, sweetie, but I just feel like I need to get a quick chest x-ray. Is that OK?" "Sure", she said. Her x-ray showed that her entire left lung was full of cancer. She had lymphoma. We found her an oncologist, and she was cured within a few months.

We had an eighteen-year-old boy with a history of congenital heart disease who came in with "cold symptoms". Within two minutes of sitting in triage, he slumped over and became unconscious and pulseless in his stretcher. We rushed him into the critical care area of the ER. We started chest compressions, intubated him, drew blood, got IV access, and did all the necessary life-saving things. His mother watched us while we performed CPR on her son. Normally we don't allow this, but unfortunately his mother had seen this same occurrence before just a few years prior. She stood there praying and told us we were doing a good job and to just keep going. She said her son was strong and he would survive this. "He's done it before, and today, he'll do it again. Come on, Demitrius. Come on, baby. Wake up. You got this, baby. Wake up. I know you will, baby. Come on, now." We could tell she believed her words. His pulse returned, and he became conscious within a few minutes of CPR. We brought him back to life. We flew him to another hospital in a helicopter. I remember him saying "thank you" past the tube in his lungs as we pushed him out the door to the ambulance bay.

Shortly after that, I treated a twenty-year-old kid for a staph infection in his thumb. It was an easy diagnosis, and I didn't spend much time with him. That must have been the best damn ten minutes of his life because later that night, while browsing the "men for women" section on the local Craigslist website, one of my nurses came across a peculiar post titled "Decatur ER". The post read as follows:

"To ER PA #672" (that's me!) "You are one hot momma. Thanks for being on *staph* in the ER tonight".

On one hand, I found this super creepy and contemplated calling the police because we had a stalker in our midst. On the other hand, how clever is it that he said "*staph*"!? For some reason, I am routinely asked out on dates by men who present to the emergency department with antecubital abscesses from shooting up methamphetamine or men who have originally come in to ask me to check out their penile drip because they think they have venereal disease. I pass no judgement on any of them and, in fact, admire their bravery, but I am not interested in going on dates with them. So, I just tell them I'm actually into chicks.

We treated an eight-month-old that had been repetitively kicked by her stepfather and then thrown against a wall. The child had multiple long bone and skull fractures. She also had a brain bleed. She came in alive, and we flew her out alive. She lived, but she ended up with massive developmental delays. We have taken care of babies whose names we did not know who were found in the middle of fields. Some lived. Some did not. I have seen so many pediatric traumas caused by so-called "loved ones". Pediatric cardiac arrests are the worst. Most cardiac arrests end in death, and there is nothing we can do about it. When it happens to adults, we are generally able to pick up and continue on to the next patient and delay mourning until our shifts are over. When it happens to children, we try and do the same, but it never works. Someone breaks down, which causes all of us to break down. Some days it doesn't seem like it, but we're human, too. We care. That's why we do this. We love people. We love our jobs. We love our patients, every one of them, from the sweet old lady to the drunk, belligerent man who tried to hit us. We know you are at your lowest low when you come to see us. We get it.

We heard a call over the radio that said EMS was en route with a 22 year old male who had been the victim of a gunshot wound ten minutes prior. This happened a week after Corey died. The patient was a beautiful young man. We were unable to resuscitate him. We could tell from his wounds that the bullets had ripped through his aorta. He was shot over a road rage incident. His little brother was in the car with him and watched the incident take place. I cried for a day over that boy. It was so hard to lose someone so young, especially after I had just lost my brother. Two years later, I was working in the fast track, and an equally handsome boy came in for a small knee laceration. While I was suturing him up, I noticed a tattoo on his arm that said "Nicholas" and a date. I said, "Who is your tattoo for, honey?"

Boy: "My brother. He died here two years ago. It's been really hard on me. I was in the car when it happened." I couldn't believe it. This handsome young man was the little brother of the boy we tried to save a few years ago.

Me: "I saw your brother that day. He was so handsome and so brave. I cried about the loss of your brother. I think of him often. I'm so sorry."

Boy: (Leans over and throws his arms around me despite the needle in my hand) "I knew it! I knew there was a reason for me coming here! Tell me you did everything you could! You did, didn't you?"

Me: "Yes, of course we did. I had just lost my brother one week prior. He was only a little older than Nicholas. We worked very hard to save your brother. We did absolutely everything that we could, honey".

I maintained a bit of a relationship with that boy. He came to visit to tell me about his life's accomplishments sometimes. He had run into a lot of trouble since his brother's death, and I encouraged him to make a better life for himself. His mother was grateful for our relationship. It was therapeutic for all of us.

Amanda was a drug addict. I saw her for a small laceration also. She asked me for narcotics for her tiny laceration. I told her that I had seen her several times before, and I never give her narcotics, and today wasn't going to be the day either. I told her I was afraid she was addicted to them. I told her I didn't give them to her because I cared about her. I told her it was "tough love", and that she wouldn't get narcotics from me. I told her to care about herself because I cared about her. I told her I would be available to help her if she ever decided to get clean. It was the same spiel I give to all of my drug addicted patients. I have a special place in my heart for them. I have been around it all my life. Amanda returned to see me six months later. I had long forgotten about the encounter by then.

Amanda: "Marlee, I'm not here for an ER visit. I'm here to tell you that you took care of me six months ago. Since I left here that day, I have not touched another drug. I came to tell you because you gave me motivation. You told me you cared about me, and I hadn't heard that from anyone for years. I am so thankful for you, and I want you to have this. It's my 24 hours sober coin. It has been the most important accomplishment I've ever made in my life, and I want you to have it.

Me: "Aw! I'm honored you would think to give it to me. I am so proud of you, but I think you should keep your coin because it is so important to you."

Amanda: "No. You have to take it. Please." She shoved the coin into my hand and closed my fingers around it.

I ultimately took the coin. Amanda returned in another month to tell me she had written me a poem about how I was her angel. It was three pages long. I was so grateful. I haven't seen her since then, but I hope she is doing okay. Part of me worries that she hasn't come around because maybe she's fallen off the wagon again. I carry Amanda's coin with me during every shift.

Joshua was seven, and he was deathly afraid of needles. He had fallen at the playground and needed sutures in his head. I'm not a believer in knocking kids out with drugs to suture them. Joshua's mother mentioned in passing that he loved music. I told Joshua that if he felt anything he didn't like, he could tell me to stop, and we could take a break. I also told him that if he did a good job, I would sing the whole time. Joshua didn't know I could sing, but he was curious to find out. I started injecting, and he said he was okay and for me to start singing. "Somewhere over the rainbow. Way up high..." Joshua was asleep by the end of the song. I was amazed that it actually worked. I scored major points with his mother, who later brought me cupcakes.

There are so many stories I could tell. Another book, perhaps. These people who tell me I've made such a difference in their lives have no idea what a difference they make in mine every single day.

Derek and I had finally had a few good months together, so he asked me to marry him. We had dated for five years. I said yes. I loved him. There was never a question in my mind about that. We invited all of our friends and family to the wedding. This included my mother. I hadn't spoken to her for about a year prior to that. She visited us in Alabama and didn't speak very highly of my husband-to-be. I tolerated it. She attempted to cook something (for the first time in our lives), and she realized I didn't own a stock pot. She said, "You know what. I'm going to take you and buy you a stock pot.

117

Every woman needs a stock pot!" "Mom, I'm fine. I don't really cook. I can buy my own stock pot if it becomes a necessity". I was making four times her salary by then. "No. I insist. Get in the car." Off we went, to Walmart, to buy a gigantic pot. I really don't like Walmart. I think it's an excellent concept. I just get terrible anxiety when I hear that the plan is to go there. I have an unrealistic fear that someone is going to crash into me with their buggy or something, and it's going to be like a buggy duel in the middle of the aisle. It doesn't make sense, but it is a very real fear of mine. There are lots of people, and there is lots of indoor traffic with lots of mental stimulation, and people let their children run amok. It's all just very overwhelming.

During the drive, my mother reminded me how it was crazy that I was going to eventually be a wife with no stock pot and how that wasn't acceptable and how she was going to get me the best stock pot Walmart had to offer and how she was the greatest mother ever for buying me kitchenware. We made it to the parking lot, and she parked the car. She said one more thing, which I can't remember, and all the anger that had built up within me over the past 26 years came out at once. I told her I didn't want a fucking pot and that I didn't need her. And I never needed her because I never actually *had* her and that she was like a slow poison, and she was killing me, and that she needed to leave. Today. Now! She was very offended that I had finally snapped. I don't remember anything she said, but I remember her packing her things and taking a slow, exaggerated, dramatic walk out my front door. I slammed that door so fast it might have actually hit her in the ass. I still don't own a stock pot, but I'm doing just fucking fine.

I invited my mother to my wedding because I thought it was appropriate. I felt bad for treating her the way I did, but I also thought it was finally necessary to tell her how I felt, but I absolutely knew that we would not ever be having any kind of relationship really. She was excited about the invite because she sent me engagement gifts: two hand-puppet back scrubbers (one was a male frog, and the other a female

118

frog) and two wine glasses from the dollar store. I know it's the thought that counts, but I would rather have had nothing. The wine glasses were cute, but I hadn't drunk wine since my communion, and she knew that. I laughed at the back scrubbers. They were ridiculous, and the whole idea was ridiculous.

My wedding day was beautiful. It was everything I had ever imagined. Derek cried while reading his personalized vows. He stayed sober the whole time per my request. I promised him he could drink as much as he wanted on the honeymoon if he behaved at our wedding. If you ever find yourself making such negotiations during your wedding planning, you may want to insert yourself a different groom. Derek did have champagne during the toast, and he finished my glass after I took my sip, but I think that was all he had. I danced with my new father-in-law to *Tupelo Honey*. It was a tribute to my mother because it was her favorite song. I winked at her when it came on, and she bawled her eyes out. My father-in-law walked me down the aisle. I loved that man. He was only half as judgmental as his wife, but he grew to love me. He had a heart attack a few years prior, and I was there for him. He said he was not going to have emergency surgery, and I leaned over his bed with tears in my eyes, grabbed his hand and said, "Too fucking late. The ambulance is already on their way to take your stubborn ass. You're going." I worked at the hospital he went to, so I had connections. I made the ER doc call the cardiologist even though my father-in-law initially refused transfer to the facility that could do the procedure necessary to save his heart. He was dying, and I saw it. His oldest sons (including my husband) were too inebriated to realize that he was dying. His wife was in shock. It was like standing in the room with a bunch of zombies trying to get them to make a decision, so I made it for them. They did the surgery, and he was fine. The boys almost got kicked out of the hospital that night for acting like idiots in the intensive care unit. They were walking around with half-drunk beer cans in their back pockets and slamming doors out of anger. I left Derek there with no ride home.

About nine months after my wedding, my mom underwent a series of surgeries. I believe she had gastric bypass surgery then had her gallbladder removed weeks later. I really didn't know because I had maintained the "we will not have a relationship" mindset after my wedding. I felt like I could love her better from far away. Even the sound of her voice eventually made me cringe. I couldn't talk to her on the phone. I was so angry with her for so many reasons, even after some pretty intensive therapy. One day, I got a call from Rachel, "Mom is really sick. I'm taking her back to the hospital. She's acting really weird."

Me: "She always acts weird. What's the deal?"

Rachel: "No I'm serious. Something is wrong."

Me: "OK, well take her in and see what's up. Keep me posted."

My sister told me that her doctor took one look at her and admitted her to the hospital. Apparently she was bleeding from her stomach, so they did another surgery to try and stop the bleeding. They said she coded on the table twice, but only for thirty seconds each time. They were able to resuscitate her each time. They were unsure whether or not they had successfully stopped the bleeding, so they decided to give her a blood transfusion just in case. When she came out of surgery, she vomited lots of blood. Rachel called me again, "Mar, she keeps throwing up blood. She says she's dying. She said she's gonna die! I don't know what to do. What should I do!? Is she dying!?"

Me: "She's not dying, Rachel. She's histrionic. She always has been. You know that. Try to comfort her. I'm sure she'll be alright. Keep me posted."

I didn't know the history of things that happened until after this. Apparently she actually was very sick. It was like "the boy who cried wolf" situation. My mother was always so dramatic. We never knew when to believe her and when not to.

Rachel called back. "They said they're going to sedate her and put her on a ventilator. They said it's the only way to calm her down. They said it looks like the bleeding has stopped, but they want her to be comfortable. They won't let me back in the room. They said for me to go home for the night. I told her I loved her and that I would see her tomorrow. Mom looked right at me and said 'I'm dying. I won't be here tomorrow.' I don't know what to do. Should I make them let me in there?"

Me: "Rachel, they're professionals. They know what they're doing. I don't know all the details, and it's hard for us to understand. They have to do what they think is best. Tell them they can call me about all of this."

Rachel eventually went home. She didn't go back into the room because she wasn't allowed. My mother's surgeon called me a few minutes later and told me the same story. I told him that I trusted his judgment and to do what was best for her. He told me my sister was difficult to deal with. Most people didn't know, but Rachel was very much addicted to prescription drugs at that point. I told him she was very afraid and to please be good to her. I told him I could explain things better to her now that I understood.

The following morning, nurses told my sister that my mother was unresponsive. They said sometimes this happened with patients who were intubated and sedated, but the difference was that my mother's pupils were nonreactive. They called the neurologist, and she did an EEG on my mother. No brain activity. In the medical community, brain death is death. People have a hard time understanding this. I had a hard time understanding how my mom was talking the night before and woke up brain-dead after just being put on a ventilator. I suppose it could happen because it did, but it was bizarre. I explained to my family that it was now only machines and medication that was keeping our mother alive. We would soon be taking her off life support. None of my other siblings except Rachel would be able to get there in time. I told her to put the phone up to my mother's ear.

Me: "Mom. I want you to know that I love you. And that I've always loved you. And that despite all the things that have happened, I respect you. You have always been my hero. I love you. And it's OK with me if you want to just go. We will be fine. Rachel will be fine. Go."

My mother had never been the same since my brother died. I imagine she caught one glimpse of him in the afterlife and ran like hell toward him. Rachel called my other brothers and had each of them say their goodbyes similarly. Then, Rachel bravely told the doctors that she was ready to let my mother go. She said my mom's heart pumped for two minutes after she was extubated. That is a very long time when you're waiting for someone's heart to beat for the last time. She said although she was extremely sad, there was peace in the room. When it is expected, death is usually a peaceful thing. It's when we try and intervene with machines and yelling and alarms that it becomes hectic. I have been present for the death of many others' loved ones. Sometimes I have been among the only ones in the room to act as a "loved one". Sometimes we have to be the ones to hold their hands when their families can't get there. And sometimes they don't have anybody, so we play with their hair and hold their hands and sing to them. Or we tell jokes. It's surprising how many people want to laugh when they're dying. I imagine I'll be one of them. Death is a beautiful thing when it's done right. Death is the one inevitable thing we're promised in life.

My mother was determined to be brain-dead on my little sister's birthday. She was extubated two days later. She

122

died in a room full of all the family who could get there in time. The room was packed out. She was an old intensive care nurse. Every day, she had taken care of patients on ventilators. She watched many people breathe their last breaths. None of us thought she would go like that.

My mother was not afraid to die. She spoke openly about it. She talked about how she wanted her funeral to be, what she wanted in her obituary, what songs she wanted played at the wake, how despite her many failures in life, she loved God, and she was going to Heaven. She told us that we would know when she got there because we would receive flowers shortly after her death. On the day of her funeral, the man she was dating at the time, a man whom I'd never seen and never even known existed, walked up to me and handed me a rose. He walked away without saying anything. We threw a huge party on my mother's behalf. They took shots of *red headed sluts* out of syringes in her honor. We danced with our brothers to *Simple Man* because that's what she always sang to them. It was a beautiful day. She was buried in a gorgeous silver coffin that was ultimately topped with over 300 roses by the time it was in the ground. I remember a huge group of hippie college students walking into the funeral parlor together. All of them were crying. I had never seen any of them before. I asked Rachel who they were. "Oh. After work, mom would go down to the 'Occupy Pittsburgh' rallies and take care of the people there. Those are some of the people she helped". They told me my mother was an inspiration because she encouraged them to follow their dreams and to speak up and never take shit from anyone. They told me she was such a badass. She was.

A few months later, while working in the ER, a nurse told me we had a new patient. This woman had never been there before, and she was complaining about some nonsense that the nurse couldn't really understand. I brushed this off because it's actually pretty common for us to have no clue why people come to the ER. I walked into the room to find a lady, about 60 years old, with white-blonde hair and gorgeous blue eyes sitting on the stretcher in a gown. She looked strikingly like my mother. She stared at me for what seemed like an unnecessarily long amount of time before she spoke, but she smiled the whole time. "Mrs. Jones, I'm Marlee. I'm one of the PAs here in the ER, and I'm going to be taking care of you, OK? What brings you to our ER today?" Mrs. Jones still didn't speak for a few awkward seconds. She stared at me. I thought she was trying to steal my soul with her eyeballs. "I have...um...my throat hurts. Haaaa!" I tried to get the rest of her history from her, but she spent most of the time smiling and laughing at her own words. I remember thinking I would be adding a drug screen to her labs. I thought she was crazy. I leaned over her to do her physical exam, and I smelled Angel perfume, my mother's signature scent. This was getting too bizarre for me, but I told her, "You're wearing Angel. That was my mother's signature scent". She laughed again. She reached up and touched my hair and she cupped her hands around my face and said, "Your mother loved you very much, Miss Marlee. I imagine she'd be proud of you in here doing all of this." I freaked the fuck out. I tried to leave the room smoothly, but I'm sure she could tell I was completely frazzled. I went to the bathroom for a few minutes to talk myself out of believing what I thought had just happened. I passed my nurse in the hall on the way out. "Where did that lady go?" "What lady?" "The one with the bullshit story. The crazy one!" "Oh my God. Are you serious?" I went into the room. The bed was unmade, and the gown the patient was wearing lay across it. "No fucking way. Did anyone see that lady leave?" Everyone looked at me like I was nuts. "The lady who was in here. Where did she go?" No one knew.

I didn't cry about my mother's death until I saw her in her coffin on the day of her funeral. And even then, I only cried for about two minutes. I haven't cried about it since. It's her fault that I didn't cry very much. She made me this tough. Some days I feel like there were still things I needed to learn from her, but most days, I realize how she prepared me for real life. In the weeks after my mother's death, I started to realize why she may have done some of the things she did. It's easy to forgive someone when they're no longer here. Getting older allows us to realize that sometimes we have to do what we know has to be done without explaining it to anyone else. The lack of explanation allows people to make their own assumptions about our personal decisions, even when they don't know all the facts. I was guilty of such assumptions for most of my life when it pertained to my mother. I was young and inexperienced. Grudges force us to focus on negatives. Forgiveness clears our minds. Even when I had to convince myself that I did not, I loved my mother. Every bit of my independence, my poise, my silver tongue; it's all because of her.

"Our fate lies in the things we love, and sometimes the things we love are the things that lead us in the destruction of ourselves."

-R.M. Drake

Relationshit

I was divorced from my ex-husband in under two years of being married to him. One night, after watching the Super bowl at a friend's house, Derek again started to belittle me and call me names. It was just something he did after drinking all night, but this time, he did it in front of people, and I was embarrassed. We got home, and I went to bed. I had become exhausted from many nights of arguing with him while he was drunk, and I'd learned my lesson about trying to talk it out while he was under the influence. It never got us anywhere. I was awakened to the sound of my dog squealing. Derek had the dog hanging in the air by one hand and was beating her with the other.

Me: "Put her down! Now!"

Derek: "She pissed on the floor!"

Me: "She's a puppy. That's what they do. It's a tile floor! I'll clean it. There are other ways to discipline her. Put her down." He hit her again. I threw a decorative porcelain ball against the wall about 10 feet from him. He says I was trying to hit him. I was an all-star pitcher in softball. If I want to hit you with a ball, I will. He dropped the dog.

Me: "That is IT. I can't take it anymore. I want a divorce!" I ran into our bedroom and slammed and locked the door. I had never said this to him before, and I meant it. And he knew it. He burst through the door, breaking the door jam.

Derek: "You want a divorce, bitch!? Fine!" He had a metal slinky in his hand. I have no idea why he chose to use that, but he bashed that metal slinky against the bridge of my nose. I felt blood running down my face. I saw stars, not because he hit me hard enough, but because I was infuriated that he hit me. I started to dial 9-1-1. He grabbed my phone and smashed it on our dresser over and over until it was broken and wouldn't turn on. I ran into the bathroom and looked at my face. I stared at myself in the mirror for what felt like a long time. And I said out loud: "This is what your life has become. This is where you live. This is what you are allowing yourself to be." Derek was already gone. He left the house and went to his parents'. I was disgusted with myself. I had known it was only a matter of time before that had happened. I don't remember the next few days except that I was without a phone and had to lie to everyone at work the next day about how my dog somehow massacred my nose. I wondered if people actually believed me. And do you believe I actually went back to trying to be a wife? I was in love, and I was used to carrying on despite things going badly. During that time, I never told anyone that happened. I remember thinking "What am I going to say? I have to get a divorce because I got smashed in the face with a child's toy?" It was an embarrassing thing to have to say, but abuse is abuse, and it comes in all different forms. Derek did tell his mother what happened. She came to my house unannounced and uninvited to talk to me about what had happened that night. Then she said, "You know...being hit by your husband isn't the worst thing that could happen." And I said, "And that is one of the many ways in which you and I differ." She told me that if I was going to divorce her son to make it quick and not to drag it out. I told her that if I decided to do that, I would not drag it out. She did cry that day on my couch. I could tell she was disappointed in her son. I could tell she felt something for me. That was the last time I ever saw her.

Even though I tried to continue being a wife, something changed that night. I learned to love myself more than I loved him. I opened my eyes wide and saw things for what they were. We had both made mistakes, but I eventually convinced myself that I was living a life that I didn't approve of. So, without any advice or input from friends or family, I planned my escape. I knew I had to get out. I knew things would never change. I had spent thousands of dollars on marriage counseling for the both of us, counseling both together and separate, about issues within our marriage and other issues. I visited some friends in Montana and eventually decided to move there. My divorce was finalized within a month of filing, just like I promised my ex mother-in-law. I thought he got a pretty good deal. I refused to be one of those "crazy ex-wives" who took everything and left. I work with ER doctors, and those fools get divorced all the time. I've heard their stories. That divorce was one of the hardest things I've ever gone through. Actually deciding that it is necessary to separate yourself from the person you love most must be one of the hardest things people can do. I had become quite practiced at separating myself from people I love, but I had never loved anyone like I loved him. I didn't stop loving him after that night he hit me. It took a while for that. I just stopped respecting him because I had to start respecting myself. I really feel for people who have to leave abusive relationships with no resources. I had a good career and a little extra cash. I can't imagine having to get out with nothing. People do it, though. They are stronger than me. It's a terrible thing to live in fear of your own well-being knowing that someone you love may become violent with you. I hear people tell victims of domestic abuse to "just get out". It's not that simple. I didn't understand it until it happened to me. And I imagine, like most other things, that's the way it is for most people. Perhaps it's best to not give your opinion unless you've been there.

"If one advances confidently in the direction of his dreams, and endeavors to live the life which he has imagined, he will meet with a success unexpected in common hours."

-Henry David Thoreau

Final Thoughts

I lived in Montana for about eighteen months. I fell in love with the most wonderful man I have ever met. His name is Eric. He is 6'2", muscular, handsome, and he has a beard. He respects me. We have been married for almost two years, and I have never once questioned his morals or his love for me. He opens my car door and washes the dishes. He is incredibly funny. He is a total nerd but is more of a badass than I am! Thanks to him, I now know several jiujitsu moves and can answer many trivia questions about superheroes. I also play Dungeons and Dragons. My character is a charismatic, slutty rogue assassin with tattoos and a foul mouth.

I have fallen in love with myself. This amazing thing happened to me when I turned thirty. I stopped giving a shit about everyone else's expectations and started really living for me. I feel like I am unstoppable. I meditate every day. I do yoga. I have started a blog (www.pagypsy.com). I write something almost every day. I paint. I sing. I dance. I do whatever the fuck I want, whenever I want. We moved to Pensacola, Florida, but we regularly return to vacation in Montana because a piece of Eric's heart still lives there. We travel as often as we can. I absolutely love our life.

On February 13th, 2017, we gave birth to a beautiful red-haired, blue-eyed baby girl. Her name is Rebel Abriel Fenner. People have told me all my life that having children is the best thing they've ever done. I have done a lot of things and have always thought those people were just saying that, but they're right. For a long time after I found out we were having a girl, I was worried because of the strained relationship I had with my mother. Rebel and I are going to be just fine. I didn't know love until I met her. Thank you for that, Baby Girl.

I am so grateful for this extraordinary life that I have been able to live. Or maybe it isn't extraordinary at all. Maybe this is just life, for everyone. Everybody has their shit. Most people just don't write books about it. I'm thankful for all of the people who have influenced me and allowed me to be the person I am today. I am thankful that people have convinced me that my life is interesting and that I should write a book. It has been a therapeutic experience. I am thankful for the good times, but I'm mostly thankful for the bad times. That is when we learn the most. Getting through the tough times lets you know how resilient you really are, and that builds strength and character. I'd rather fall into a sewer and come out smelling like a rose than be bathed in the finest essence all my life and stay that way forever. That seems boring to me.

This is the true story of my life so far. Despite my many faults and failures, I am proud of the person I have become. I have learned that no matter what happens, life goes on. It is up to you to determine how it will go on. You are the master of your decisions. You determine your own fate. I have learned that attitude is everything. If you remain optimistic about things, they will inevitably turn out in your favor, even if it doesn't seem that way initially. I have learned to never judge a book by its cover. Some of the most interesting, most creative, most caring people I have met are those who may fit into the category of "strange" or "eclectic" or "awkward". I have learned to always encourage people to be who they are and to take control of their own lives. You never know what battles other people are fighting. You never know whose life you will change by simply offering to allow them to be comfortable being themselves, to tell someone you will be there for them no matter what. You never know who you will inspire by making decisions to better your own life. I've learned to pay little attention to the opinions of others when it pertains to my own life decisions. As far as we know, we have one chance to be here, and sometimes life turns out to be painfully short. We might as well be as happy as we can while it lasts. There isn't a person in the world who knows what is better for you than you do.

In my line of work, we are reminded every day that life is a precious gift, and that it can be stripped from us at any moment. Always love fully. Forgive quickly. Say everything you need to say as soon as you think of it. Ask everything you need to ask as soon as you feel like it's necessary to know. None of us are promised a tomorrow.

Above all, care for others, no matter what. Sometimes those people who seem the most wretched are those who need your love most. Even if you can't stand to be around them, love them. Care for them. Forgive them. There is nothing in the world that will fill your heart more than being selfless. And always remember to remain true to yourself. Remember you are the one person you have to answer to on a daily basis. And on those days you find that you're imperfect, forgive yourself. We are all imperfect, and that is what makes life exciting.

I am the bastard daughter of a whore and a heroin addict. I mean that in the most endearing way possible. I have stood over two miles high on a mountain and have dove the depths of the ocean. I have healed the sick and held the hands of the dying. I have peeled myself off of the floor, drenched in tears, wiped my face, and carried on with my day. I have buried both parents, all my grandparents, many friends, and a brother. I have answered the phone on two separate occasions and have been told that my baby sister has died of a heroin overdose. Both times after calling the coroner's office, I learned that thankfully that wasn't true. Keep fighting, my sweet Rachel.

I have been married and divorced and married again. Every day, I get to look at a tiny human who is made half of me and half of the man I love most in the whole world. This is a beautiful life. I am living proof that anyone can make it, no matter her circumstances. It is so important to try and have a positive attitude. I think that we are all products of what has happened to us, but I don't think that has to be a bad thing. I think that if we stare our problems in the face rather than run from them, we are better for it. If we refrain from taking ourselves so damn seriously, we are better for it. And if we remember that dealing with unfortunate, uncomfortable occurrences makes us better, more exciting people, we are better for it. I am such a proponent of remembering where I've been and where I came from. I wouldn't want to erase one second of my life or change one thing that has happened.

I am thirty-two years old, and all my dreams have come true. Everything else is just a bonus.

"If there is something you must know before I let you go, it is this:
In your journey, you will meet broken people, hateful people, and people who have lost the sight for glory.
And the beauty of it all is this:
I will tell you to love them more. To love them deeply and show them how some of us still care.
Never give up on them. For to give up on them is to destroy a reflection of ourselves."

-R.M. Drake

Genesis

Mr. Donahue was admitted to the behavioral health unit. It turns out he was having manic episodes, probably from shooting up methamphetamine. He had apparently turned to this as a coping mechanism the first time his girlfriend cheated. I don't know how long he stayed in our hospital that time. I have seen him several times since. He is much better behaved when he comes in now. I think the naked leg injection traumatized him, and I'm sorry about that. He asks me out for coffee or dinner or whatever he can get every time he comes in. I usually just get him a cup of coffee and talk with him for a few minutes in his concrete-walled ER room. He is still dating the same girl and has clearly not learned his lesson. To each his own.

Evan had appendicitis. He had emergency surgery and recovered quickly. He was able to go home early the following morning. The surgeon told me he was a very brave young man, brave like Optimus Prime.

I never saw Hank's wife break down that day in my emergency department. I imagine she held it together all day until she got home and had to lay in that bed alone. The following day, at 3:00pm, another 41 year old male came in after dropping dead about three hours after saying he had chest pain. We did not know this man's name for hours. He was homeless. We found out who he was when another man who ran the local homeless shelter became concerned that one of his tenants never came home that evening. He called the ER looking for his tenant, but he was not a family member, so we were unable to give him any information. The tenant's name was Jacob. He had no friends or family, and no one ever came to claim his body. Later that night, a black Labrador retriever continuously walked past our automatic ER doors causing them to open. After about two hours of this, the head nurse decided to bring him in. He had no collar. He hung out with us for the rest of that shift. We called him Jacob. I don't know what ended up happening to either Jacob.

Shortly after our interrupted conversation, Mrs. Reed and her son decided to take Mr. Reed off life support. It required a little more explaining and a call to the vascular surgeon at a hospital two hours away "just to make sure" he definitely wasn't going to pull through. The surgeon declined the transfer stating the patient's dissection was inoperable and incompatible with life. Sometimes people just aren't ready to let go. I imagine it is especially difficult after 73 years of marriage. We extubated Mr. Reed in the emergency department and gave him a decent amount of pain medication through his IV at the request of his family. We found him a nice, quiet room on the third floor of the hospital. Mr. Reed died in the arms of his concerned wife and beautiful son twenty two minutes after leaving our department. One day prior, he'd caught the biggest fish of his life. He was 91 years old.

Made in the USA
San Bernardino, CA
06 November 2017